A Dictionary of
Scientific Terms on Kālidāsa Literature

A Dictionary of Scientific Terms on Kālidāsa Literature

Compiled and Edited by

Jagatpati Sarkar

Foreword by

Prof. Arun Kumar Biswas

Kaveri Books

New Delhi-110002

A Dictionary of Scientific Terms on Kālidāsa Literature

First Published in 2022

ISBN: 978-81-955493-6-8

Published by

Kaveri Books

4832/24, Ansari Road

New Delhi-110002 (India)

Tel: 011-23288140, 47072321

E-mail : info@kaveribooks.com

kaveribooks@gmail.com

Website: www.kaveribooks.com

Laser Typesetting by

Aarti Computers, Delhi

PRINTED IN INDIA

Dedicated
to
my father

Late Subhankar Sarkar

Foreword

Dr. Jagatpati Sarkar and Santanu Saha have teamed up to compile an elegent dictionary of science-related words of the great poet Kālidāsa. They are specialists in the fields of Sanskrit (Inscription) and Chemistry respectively and colleagues in the world-renowned Asiatic Society, Kolkata, hallowed with the memories of great orientalists such as William Jones, Horace Wilson and James Princep etc.

I myself worked in this Society as the Mahendralal Sircar Research Professor in the History of Science (1996-2001) and worked with Jagatpati on the theme of scientific consciousness of the great poet Kālidāsa. Therefore it gives me great pleasure to write this Foreword on the mini-dictionary of Kālidāsa's scientific words.

It is meaningless to discuss science related words to Kālidāsa's era without some measure of scholarly agreement, if not unanimity, on the vexed question of Kālidāsa's time and place. What was era? The great poet of modern India, Gurudev Rabindranath Tagore wrote pithily:

Hāyre, kobe kete gache Kālidaser kāl,
Panditerā vivad kare laye tarikh sāl.
Hāriye gache se sob abdo, itivritta ache stabdha--
Geche yadi āpad geche, mithyā kolāhal.

The scholars fiercely debate amongst themselves on the era of Kālidāsa, the nuisance (apada) which is out of sight and the din is vain (mithyā). We, the historians of Science do not agree with the great poet that the issue of debate has been a nuisance and the din is vain.

There are two strong views on Kālidāsa's date. The first refers to Kālidāsa I as belonging to the first century before Jesus Christ, the city of Ujjani and the region of King Vikrāmāditya I, the Śākāri, who vanquished the Sakas or Skythians and established a new era in his time: Vikramābda or Śakābda on 58 BC. The 'first' Kālidāsa must have written the drama Mālāvikāgnimitra, the hero of which Agnimitra belonged to the Sunga dynasty (184-72 B.C.). The great dramatist poet Kālidāsa also composed two other dramas Vikramorvaśiyam and Avijnāna Śakuntalam and two poetical works Meghadutum and the first eight cantos of Kumāra Saṃbhavam (Mallinath annotated these first eight cantos and not following ones: 9th-17th, which must have keen composed later).

The second view about Kālidāsa's date veers around the reign of Chandragupta Vikramaditya II (375-413 AD) of the Gupta Era (320-480 AD) when the capital of the empire was not Ujjaini of the West but Kusumpur/Pataliputra (modern Patna) of the East. Whereas the earlier pre-Christian culture at Ujjaini was distinctly Saivite (Siva-cult), Kālidāsa II dwelt in his famous Raghuvaṃśa on the Vaisnava glory of Lord Visnu/Rama; and very little on Siva. The poet of Raghuvaṃśa described in the forth cantos (4.36-4.81) how the fourth century A.D. Hunas were defeated by the mighty emperors of the Gupta era.

The two views related to Kālidāsa I and Kālidāsa II are both correct; as a matter of fact theme was the third one as well. The third Kālidāsa might have composed the poems of less calibre: Ṛtusaṃhāra, Sṛngārāsṭakam and belonged to the dubious legend of nine jewels (intellectuals). The list of 'nine' included Kālidāsa I (apart from the famous Āryabhaṭa (b. 476 AD, his work dated 499 A.D.), Varāhamihira (work dated 505 A.D.), Skandagupta the last famous Gupta emperor had died in 780 A.D.

So when we see the so-called *Collected Works of Kālidāsa*, we should expect a bit of history of science in ancient India spanning seven centuries (1st century B.C. to 6th century AD.), more during the first century B.C. to the fourth century A.D.

It is very significant that all the three dramatic compositions of Kālidāsa I, penned during the pre-christian era, extolled Aṣṭamurti Śiva, the Lord with eight manifestations: kṣiti, ap, teja, maruta, vyoma, hotri (later mentioned as dikṣita brahmana or ātmā, soul), candra and surya. Under the Greek influence, the last three, including the 'soul' were dropped from the materialist peripatetic Aristotelian concept of the universe. Viṣnu Purāṇa and Vāyu Purāṇa also belonged to the pre-christian era. The latter specialised in several categories of Vāyu of wind: parābaha, paribaha, subaha, sambāha, udbāha, prabāha and ābaha. Avijnāna Śakuntalam (7.06) specifically mentioned the descent of King Dusyanta's chariot from the terrestrial wind or prabāha zone down to the earthly wind or ābaha zone. The common word ābhāwā (climate) has been derived from ābaha.

The 4th century A.D. Raghuvaṃśa of Kālidāsa II does not mention astamurti or the eight forms of Lord Śiva or aṣṭadhātu, an eight-element metallic alloy, but only five peripatetic elements or pancabhuta (Raghuvaṃśa, 4.11). Āryabhaṭa, the great mathematician and astronomer accepted only the first four and not vyoma, the fifth, which cannot be comprehended through our sense perceptions.

In compilation of this dictionary, the author has listed many terms related to ancient astronomy, geography, natural resources, botanical and agricultural products, minerals and metals and so on. These can be related to the time and places to which the three Kālidāsas belonged. For example we find fuller description of Ujjaini and Vidisā in Mālāvikāgnimitra, Meghduta, etc. of the Himalaya region in Kumārasaṃbhava and the Ganga-Son river area in Raghuvaṁśa. The last composition describes larger segment of the sub-continent and even an aerial view of very large tracts as if aeroplane had been discovered at that time. However the point is that such a description could not come from an author in the pre-Christian era.

Similarly, Kālidāsa I could profusely mention the indigenously available gem material vaidurya (beryl) but not the imported (from Egypt or Miśar) variety masaragalu (or marakata emerald) because the trade started during the post-christian Roman era only. The well-appreciated works on minerals, metals and gems in ancient India executed by my wife and myself, drew substantial support from the Vijnāna Chetanā in the Kālidāsa literature. We were able to compile a dictionary of Sanskritic words related to minerals, metals and gems in ancient India and are quite confident that similar vocabulary of Sanskritic words can be collated in the other categories such as flora and fauna in ancient India for which the Kālidāsa literature would be distinctly useful.

In this writings of Kālidāsa's we find abundant applications of the principles of Physics, Chemistry and Engineering: reflection of sound (Kumārasaṃbhava, 6.64) of light (Avijñāna Śakuntalam, 7.32), thermal property of light rays focussed by lens (Avijñāna Śakuntalam 2,07, Raghuvaṁśa 11.21), surface tension-related spreading of oil film over water (Raghu Vaṁśa 14.38), coagulating property of specific fruit juices clarifying muddy water (Mālavikāgnimitram 2.07), gravitational force of the moon raising the sea level on the earth (Raghuvaṁśa 12.36), phosphorescence of a specific Himalayan creeper (Kumāra Sambhavam 1.10), the concept of relative velocity during motion (Avijnāna Śakuntalam 1.08, 1.09, 7.08), the concept of causality or cause-and-effect explaining scientific observation (Avijnāna Śakuntalam 7.30), Raghuvaṃśa) and so on.

It was known during Kālidāsa's era that cooling effect could be produced by the evaporation of fine particles of water and exhibiting this principle, mechanical pump-induced water cooler could be fabricated (Raghuvaṃśa 16.49). Hot forging of iron was described (Vikramorvasiyam 2.16: Raghuvaṃśa 14.33). Our dear colleague of I.I.T. Kanpur, late Professor R Balasubramaniam described how the famous corrosion-resistant Delhi Iron Pillar was fabricated by hot forging during the reign of famous Gupta emperor Chandragupta II (375-413 A.D.). Kālidāsa II also belonged to this period composing Raghuvaṃśa.

The last technical comment that I would make in this Foreword of mine is that the Kālidāsa literature dwells on not only the glorious aspect of the Science in Ancient India but also one of the causes of its downfall Kālidāsa II must be credited in this regard for having put certain telling truths in the mouth of Lord Rāma (Raghuvaṁśa (4.85. 15.50-53. 19-33 etc). Rāma regarded his wife, Sitā to be absolutely pure ('*enam anaghā iti ca abaimi*') but banished her to the seclusion of the forest, sadly succumbing to the stronger conservative opinion amongst the masses ('lokāpabādah valavāna matah'), which was like mis-interpretation of the scientific event of lunar eclipse in terms of the so-called impure contact (rāhu grāsāh malatvenaśaśino aropitā asuduhihmatah prajāvih). Even the erudite astronomer and mathematician Brahmagupta (Brahmasphuta Siddhānta 11.52) committed the same mistake, unfairly criticised Āryabhaṭ's bold scientific assertion and for this error, was later severely admonished by the great Muslim scholar Al-Biruni. Kālidāsa II anticipated the decadence and untimely decline of the scientific spirit in ancient India.

In conclusion, I strongly recommend to the readers this dictionary of science-related words of great poet Kālidāsa compiled by Dr. Jagatpati Sarkar and Santanu Saha and even take pride in doing so, since the three of us belong to the Asiatic Society, founded by the great Orientalist Sir William Jones, who initiated modern research on the literary masterpieces of Kālidāsa containing gems of scientific thoughts. I fully anticipate and welcome that the readers would send their notes of appreciation and suggestions for improvement which would enable Sarkar and Saha to improve their renderings in the future editions of this Dictionary. I wish the duo all the best and success in their professional careers and social sojourn.

Prof. Arun Kumar Biswas
Former Professor
IIT, Kanpur
& Asiatic Society, Kolkata

Abbreviation

Abhi	-	Abhijñānaśakuntalam
Kumāra	-	Kumāra Saṃbhavam
Mālā	-	Mālāvikāgnimitram
Megha	-	Meghadutam
Nalo	-	Nalodaya
Puṣpa	-	Puṣpavānavilāsa
Raghu	-	Raghuvaṃsam
Ṛtu	-	Ṛtusaṃharam
Śṛngāra	-	Śṛngāratilakam
Śrngāraṣṭa	-	Śrngāraṣṭakam
Śruto	-	Śrutodaya
Vik	-	Vikramourvaśiyam

Map of India & its outlying regions as represented in Kalidasa's works

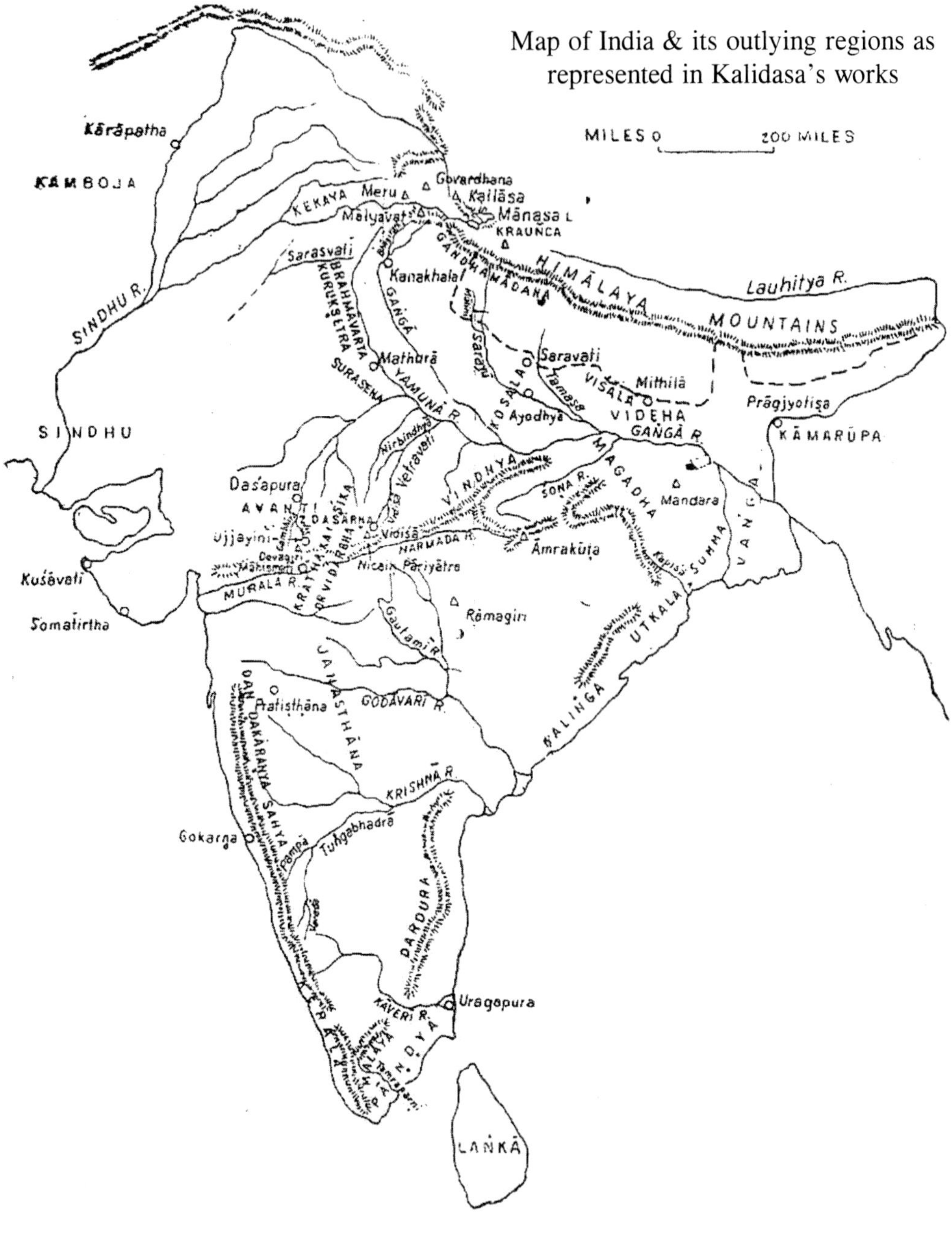

Introduction

India and China are the world's most ancient surviving civilizations of today. Human beings always desire to survive, communicate and progress. This is the inseparable idea from its existence. This has given rise to everything we can think about our civilization. As we have achievements, we also have set-backs and failures. Each mistake teaches us something new and helps us to progress in a new way. Introspective and creative society finds out better answers and solutions and this process continues as if there is no final answer to the need of the mundane world. This experience gets codified in its literature, architecture, lifestyle, law, sports, trade and performing arts and into every conceivable creation of that civilization.

Triumph of modernity tempts us to believe that all other branches of knowledge are subservient to science and technology. However science and its applications cannot be separated from the culture of the civilization.

We know Copernicus is credited for heliocentric view of the universe. This revolution is considered as the corner stone of modern science which led further to industrial revolution in the West. This is true for the Western science but insistence of pinning the beginning or creativity of astronomy and mathematics to that period makes earlier civilization apparently opaque. The invention of calculus is attributed to Newton and Leibniz. But Madhava, a 13th century Kerala mathematician has used these principles at least three centuries prior to Newton. Those were released in the text and commentaries of Kerala mathematicians of later centuries.

Many toxicological texts got translated into Arabic first from 7th to 10th century A.D. These texts acknowledge the Indian source. There are many such examples which need further research. The concept of science here should transcend beyond conventional subjects, like physics, chemistry, biology or mathematics. They should embrace science of grammar, lexicography, logic, architecture, philosophy, law and justice, commerce, administration and management. These works should be developed for further studies.

Sanskrit is one of the earliest Indo-European languages. The Ṛgveda is the earliest written record of the Indo-European languages. Sanskrit literature has been flowing like mighty river wandering through many lands. Besides purely literary matters, many philosophical, scientific and technical subjects have been dealt with in different Sanskrit works.

Kālidāsa is admittedly one amongst the greater classical poet of Sanskrit in India. His works have been studied from various stand points, viz, his similes, society, the human meaning of his poems and dramas etc. But no serious and systematic attempt has yet been made to study his words on science. The study of the words is necessary not for this purpose alone, but even to assess fully the literary value of the work, such a study is indispensable. It may be mentioned that a critical study of Kālidāsa's works has already revealed his penchant for the use of soft words even at the sacrifice of the spirit of what he describes. The study of the words, used by him, has other uses. The geographical names, occurring in his work, sometimes throw light on the topography of a country.

The plan of our work is the following. First of all, the words under each head have been arranged in the alphabetical order. Against each entry the references to the text are mentioned. The meaning of the word has been indicated; all the information have been gathered from the works of Kālidāsa. Sometimes a cluster of words has been made the basis of the meaning of the word. But in most of the cases we have tried to make an entry separately.

Professor Suresh Chandra Banerjee has composed *Kālidāsa Kosa:* a classified register of the flora, fauna, geographical names, musical instruments and legendary figures in Kālidāsa's works under Chowkhamba series, Varanasi in 1968. Of the fauna of Kālidāsa, Satyacharan Laha has studied only the birds from the ornithologist's point of view in his Bengali book *'Kālidāser Pakhi'*. Of Kālidāsa's flora, Saumyendranath Thakur has studied the flowers in his Bengali book called *'Kālidāser Kāvye Phul'*. He has noted the names of the different flowers and has given the references to the places in which these names occur. In the book *'India in Kālidāsa'*, B. S. Upadhyaya has dealt with the flora and fauna of Kālidāsa. In the portion of fauna, he does not note the scientific names of all animals and birds mentioned by Kālidāsa. *'The Geographical Data of the Raghuvaṃsa and the Daśakumaracarita'* by Mark Collins (Liepzig, 1907) mentions only a few of the geographical names found in the Raghuvaṃsa.

Kālidāsa's power of describing nature is superb. Some of the indications of the symbolism of the poet are seen in his works. Kamdhenu and Nandini are suggested as the symbols of Prakriti and Vikrti: the cosmic energy or intellect and its shadow, in individuals (Raghu 1.77). Nandini is considered as a Vidya too and it is presumed that Vasistha advised Dilipa to get both the Nandini (1) Nandini-cow and (2) Nandini-vidya (Ra III.4).

In Ṛtusaṃhara, Meghduta and Mālāvikāgnimitram, Kālidāsa depicts nature in both its forms-overt and covert, i.e., the nature of the outer world and the collective unconscious of mankind. Kālidāsa starts with the outer nature in Ṛtu and proceeds gradually towards the inner nature which reaches its peak in Raghuvaṃśa.

Kālidāsa's literature stands for eternal voice of beauty, bliss and peace which are also gifts of science for all times. And this science is applicable for all the sectors – private and public and fruitful for all the mankind.

The plan of this work started long time back. We were generally accustomed to see Kālidāsa as a powerful poet in classical Sanskrit literature. But hardly did we imagine that a glimpse of science awakening or science movement in India may be deciphered from Kālidāsa's literature. A clear idea of science knowledge has indeed been compiled by Kālidāsa in his works.

We have not gone into the disputed area of the number of Kālidāsas and their age. But we have touched almost every Kālidāsa, popular or unpopular in the sense for the completeness of the word. The idea of the different Kālidāsa's we obtained first from Professor Arun Kumar Biswas, former Professor of IIT Kanpur and former Research Professor of History of Science of the Asiatic Society, Kolkata, approximately five years ago. When we first undertook this work we started to collect the words of Kālidāsa's work related with science at random. And total words we collected were more than 2000, the idea of micro study came afterwords. The sorting of out process started and we took only science-related words and the number reached nearly 400 (approx).

We have not prepared a cluster of different subjects such as Astronomy, Natural Philosophy, Mathematics, Chemistry, Agriculture, Geology, Zoology, Botany etc., but we have tried to show the co-related words assembled together to show the exact phenomena. The distribution order of the words is alphabetical. The scientific term has also been given to the words. We have incorporated photographs in some cases, words in the exact area. The book of Professor Suresh Chandra Banerjee entitled *Kālidāsakoṣa* helped us very much. But we did not follow this book in toto. In a few cases we have rectified the statement. We have consulted the book of Ramaprasad Dwivedi entitled, *Kālidāsa Granthāvali* (Complete Works of Kālidāsa, second revised edition) and *Kālidāser Pakhi* by Satyacaran Laha. We have gone through the book *Kālidāser Kāvye Phul* by Saumendranath Thakur. The very important work of B.S. Upadhyaya named "*India in Kālidāsa's Era*" has been dealt with in our work. The *Geography of Kalidasa* by H.C. Chaklader has also been consulted in the present work.

In the realm of the past, impacts of science and technology have never been set aside. But the quantum of impact was relatively less on account of relatively lesser development of science and technology. We hope that a new form of science would be developed which may monitor and restrict the malevolent result and damage on human species. We fervently desire that the relationship and so also the interaction between science and society may turn both meaningful and useful. We take this opportunity to acknowledge our gratitude and indebtedness to Professor Pallab Sengupta, President of the Asiatic Society who was the constant force behind us in our study from start to end. We have obtained a solid support and many important suggestions from Professor Apurba K. Chattopadhyay, former teacher of Zoology of Bardhaman Raj College and our revered teacher Dr. Shyamal Kanti Chakraborty, former Director of Indian Museum and National Library, Kolkata. We are obliged to them very much. We are grateful to Professor Dr. Arun Kumar Biswas for kindly writing the Foreword for this book. He has truly inspired us in every movement.

I also acknowledge the eminent services of Dr. Santanu Saha in preparation of particularly in shaping of photographs and scientific notes on those matter very minutely.

We have every hope that scholars of Sanskrit language and literature particularly engaged in Kālidāsa will appreciate this work. Our thanks are also due to Mr. Rakesh Goel of Kaveri Books, New Delhi for his kind attention and good help for this publication.

Jagatpati Sarkar

A

Ābila (आविल)

Meaning/ Scientific term: Garbage

Description: Garbage is rubbish, especially waste from a kitchen or industry or any kind of workshop. Village waste, town waste, municipal waste etc.

Reference: Mālā - 2.7

Abja (अब्ज)

Meaning/ Scientific term: Lotus *(Nelumbo nucifera)*

Description: *Nelumbo nucifera*, known by a number of names including Indian lotus, Sacred lotus, Beans of India, Suriya Kamal, Padma, Pankaja, Blue Lotus or simply lotus, is a plant in the NeIumbonaceae family. Botanically *Nelumbo nucifera* may also be referred to by its former names, *Nclumbium spccsvm* (wild). This plant is aquatic perennial and alive to Greater India and Bangladesh, it is commonly cultivatcd in watcr gardcns. It has broad floting leaves and bright fragrant flowers. The leaves and flowers float and have long stems that contain air spaces. It has many petals overlapping in the symmetrical pattern. The root functions of the Lotus are carried out by rhizomes that fan out horizontally through the thud below the water. The round leaves are upto-50 cm in diameter. The flowers are rosy pink with little bit of white shade. The seeds are hard and dark brown in colour. They can vary in shape from round to oval to oblong. The Lotus flower opens in the morning and the petals fall in the afternoon. The lotus is the national flower of India and Vietnam. *Cultural Significance*: From ancient time the lotus has been a divine symbol in Asian traditions representing the virtues of sexual parity and non-attachment. It symbolizes divinity, fertility, wealth and knowledge. In India it is considered as the symbol of triumph. As it is rooted in the mud it can survive to regerminate for thousand of years. It represents long life, honour and good fortune. Hindus reverse it with the duraitees Vishnu and Lakshmi often portrayed on a pink in iconography. In the representation of

Vishnu as Padmanāva (Lotus navel) a lotus issues from his navel with Brahma on it. Goddes Saraswati is portrayed on a white-coloured lotus.

Reference: Raghu – 4.61

Adhityakā (अधित्यका)

Meaning/ Scientific term: Valley

Description: In geology, a valley or dale is a depression with predominant extent in one direction. A very deep river valley may be called a canyon or gorge. The term U-shaped and V-shaped are descriptive terms of geography to characterize the form of valley. Most valleys belong to one of those two main types of a mixture of them, at least with respect of the cross section of the slopes of billsises.

Reference: Raghu - 2.29, Kumāra-3.17

Ādra (आर्द)

Meaning/ Scientific term: Wet

Description: A substance saturated with liquid e.g. water, involving the use of water or any other liquid. In case of painting or potmaking or inking-not yet having dried or hardened (in case of earthen pot-making). Wet hair, wet cloth etc.

In case of weather, 'wet condition' is referred to 'rainy' weather or 'dampy' weather i.e., increases in the 'water vapour' in sourrounding air.

Reference: Abhi - 3.10, Mālā - 3.12, 3.13, Vik-4.38, 5.8 Ṛtu - 6.6, Nalo – 2.2, 2.59

Adri (अद्रि)

Meaning/ Scientific term: Mountain

Description: A mountain is a large land form that sketches above the surroundings land in a limited area usually in the form of peak. A mountain is generally steeper than tillā.

Or

A natural elevation of the earth surface rising more or less abruptly from the surroundings level and waiting an attitude relating to the adjacent elevation is impressive or movable.

Reference: Kumāra-1.52, 1.58, Raghu-6.60, 6.61, 16.70, 17.64, Megha-14, Nalo-3.32

Agni (अग्नि)

Meaning/ Scientific term: Fire

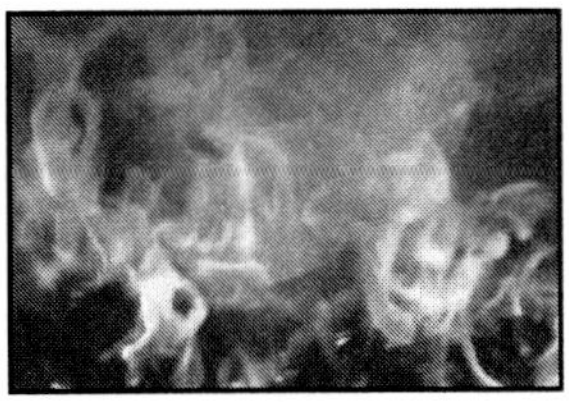

Description: Fire is the rapid oxidation of a material/substance in the chemical process of combustion, relating heat-light and various reaction products. The visible portion of fire is called flame and consists of glowing hot gases. Fire in its ost common form can result in conflagration. which has the potential top cause physical damage through burning; Fire has been used by humans for cooking, generating heat, signating and propulsion purposes.

Reference: Raghu - 1.10, 1.49, 3.12, 3.14, 8.72, 11.91, 12.56, 12.37, 45, 15.16, 17.16, 34, 19.1, Mālā - 4.12, 29, 5.17, Vik - 3, 4, 4.34, 5, 5.16, Abhi - 3.3, 4, 4.4, Ṛtu - 1.20, 1.25, Nalo - 3.17, Srngāraṣṭakam - 3

Aguru (अगुरु)

Meaning/ Scientific term: Fragrant having a pleasant odor

Description: In Hindi, it is known as "agar", which is originally Sanskrit 'aguru' (in Bengali), it is spelled 'agum'. Agarwood or oodh (or just agar) is a dark resinous heartwood that forms in *Aquilaria* and *Gyrinops,* trees (large evergreens native to southeast Asia) when they become infected with a type of mold. Prior to infection, the heartwood is relatively light and pale coloured, however as the infection progresses, the tree produces 'a dark aromatic resin' in response to the attack, which results in a very dense, dark, resin embedded heartwood. The resin embedded wood is commonly called *gaharu, jinko, aloeswood, agarwood,* or *ova'* and is valued in many cultures for its distinctive fragrance, and thus is used for incense and perfumes. The odour of agarwood is complex and pleasing, with few or no similar natural analogues. As a result, agarwood and its essential oil gained great cultural and religious significance in ancient civilizations around the world, being mentioned throughout one of the world's oldest written texts – the Sanskrit *Vedas* from India. There are fifteen species in the genus *Aquilaria* and eight are known to produce agarwood. Formation of agarwood occurs in the trunk and roots *of* trees that have been infected by a parasite ascomycetous mold, *Phaeoacremo nium parasitica*, a dematiaceous (dark-walled) fungus. As a response, the tree produces a resin high in volatile organic compounds that aids in suppressing or retarding the fungal growth, a process called tylosis. While the unaffected wood of the tree is relatively light in colour, the resin dramatically increases the mass and density of the affected wood. changing its colour from a pale beige to dark brown or black. In natural forest only about 7% of the trees are infected by the fungus. In Ayurveda the oleoresin is highly prized as well. The wood is acrid, bitter, thermogenic, digestive, carminative, deodorant, sudorific, andoyne, anti-inflammatory, antileprotic, depurative, cardiotonic, rejuvenating and tonic. It is useful in vitiated conditions of vata and kapha, halitosis, dyspepsia, anorexia, cardiac debility, skin disease, leprosy, foul ulcers, hypothermia, inflammations, rheumatoid: cough, asthma, hiccough, albuminuria and general debility. An external application of agaru is very useful in vomiting in children, pectoralgia due to pneumonia and cephalalgia. The oil is astringent, acrid, bitter. thermogenic, depurative, and anti-leprotic.

Reference: Raghu – 6.8, 8.71, 19.41, Ṛtu – 5.12

Airāvat (ऐरावत)

Meaning/ Scientific term: Elephant (1) Indian elephant - *Elephas maximus indicus,* (2) African bush elephant - *Laxadonta africana,* (3) African forest elephant - *Loxodonta cyclotis.*

Description: An elephant is a very large land animal with a long, flexible nose called a trunk, which it uses to pick up things. Elephants are in two genera of purely *Elephantidae: Elephas* and *Loxodonta.* Elephants live in India and Africa.

Reference: Raghu - 17.32, Kumāra - 3.22

Ākāś (आकाश)

Meaning/ Scientific term: Sky

Description: *See* Ambara

Reference: Vik - 1, Abhi - 6, 7.6

Akṣa (अक्ष)

Meaning/ Scientific term: Tree (*Terminalia bellirica)*

Description: A tree is a perennial woody plant. It is most often defined as woody plant that has many secondary branches supported clear of the ground on a single main stem or trunk with clear apical dominance. A tree is a plant forms that occur in many different orders and families of plants. Trees show a varity of growth forms, leaf type and shape, bark characterities and reproductive organs.

Reference: Raghu- 13.43, Kumāra - 3.46

Akṣota (अक्षट)

Meaning/ Scientific term: Walnut tree

Description: Walnuts in the nut of the trees belong to the genus *Juglans*. They are deciduous trees, 10-40 meters tall (about 30-130 ft), with pinnate leaves 200-900 was long (Alenrites triloba) with 5-25 leaflets. Walnuts is an edible nut which have a wrinkled shape and a hard sound shell that is light in colour.

Reference: Raghu - 4.69

Alakābharaṇam/Ābharaṇ (आभरण)

Meaning/ Scientific term: Sandal ornament

Description: Sandalwood is the name of different fragrant wood. The wood is heavy and yellow in colour as well as fine - groused, and unlike many other aromatic wood's retains its fragrance for decades. Sandalwood has been valued and treasured for many years for its fragrance, carving, medical and religious qualities.

Reference: Raghu - 8.62. 13.21. Vik 3 2.3, 4.33, Abhi - 4, 4.5, Ṛtu – 2.12

Alakācurna/Ālakta/Alaka (अलकाचुर्न)

Meaning/ Scientific term: Sandal paste or paste of sandlewood - Indian Sandalwood - *Santalum album*

Description: Sandalwood is the name of different fragrant wood. These woods are fielded by trees in the genus *Santalum*, which are often used for the essential oil of contains. The wood is heavy and yellow in colour as well as fine grausedm, and unlike many other aromatic wood's retains its fragrance for decades. Sandalwood has been valued and treasured for many years for its fragrance, carving, medical and religious qualities.

Reference: Mālā - 3.5, 13, Ṛtu - 4.16

Ālekhya/Abhilekha (आलेखय)

Meaning/ Scientific term: Painting/ Picture

Description: A representation of anything (of a person, a landscape, a building) upon canvas, paper or other surface, produced by means of painting, drawing, engraving, photography etc.

Reference: Raghu - 8.95, 14, 15, Ṛtu - 4.12

Ambara (अम्बर)

Meaning/ Scientific term: Sky

Description: The sky is the part of the atmosphere or of outer space visible from the surface of any astronomical objects. During day time is sky of earth has the appearance of a deep surface because of the airs scattering of sunlight.

The sky is sometimes defined as the denser gaseous part of planet's atmosphere. At night the sky has the appearance of a black surface or region scattered with stars.

Reference: Raghu – 6.67

Ambha (अम्भ)

Meaning/ Scientific term: Cloud

Description: See Ambhasā

Reference: Raghu - 17.56

Ambha (अम्भ)

Meaning/ Scientific term: Water (H_2O)

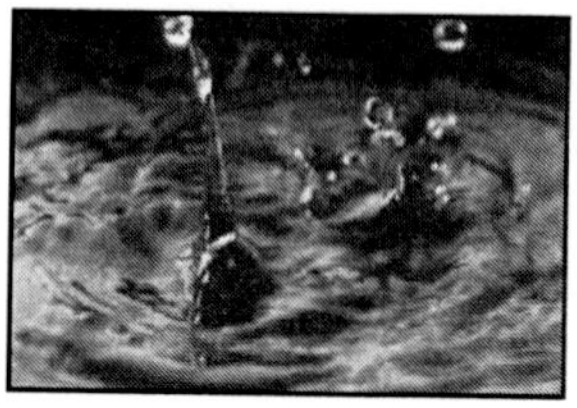

Description: Water is a clear liquid that has no colour or taste when it is pure. It falls from cloudes as rain and enters rivers and seas. All animals and people need water in order to live. Water is a chemical substance with the chemical formula H_2O. Its molecule contains one oxygen and two hydrogen atoms connected by covalent bonds. Water is a liquid at ambient conditions, but it often co-exists on Earth with its solid state, ice, and gaseous state (water vapour or steam). Water covers 70.9% of the Earth's surface. On Earth, it is found mostly in oceans and other large water bodies, with 1.6% of water below ground in aquifers and 0.001% in the air as vapor, clouds and precipitation. Oceans hold 97% of surface water, glaciers and polar ice caps 2.4%, and other land surface water such as rivers, lakes and ponds 0.6%.

Reference: Raghu – 3.53. 6.44, 9.82, 13.15, 15.58. 16.54. 16.65. 17.60, 19.9. Mālā - 3.17, Vik - 1.20, 4, Abhi - 5.12, Ṛtu - 3.17, Kumāra - 11.25, 14.13

Ambhadhara (अम्भधर)

Meaning/ Scientific term: Cloud

Description: See Ambhasā

Reference: Raghu - 6.44, 2.1, 2.17

Ambhasā (अम्भसा)

Meaning/ Scientific term: Cloud

Description: A cloud is a visible mass or droplets or little drops of water or frozen crystals suspended in the atmosphere above the surface of the Earth or another planetary body. Clouds are studied in the nephrology or cloud physics branch of meteorology.

Reference: Raghu - 11.12, Abhi - 1.27. 6.13, Ṛtu - 1.15

Ambhoja (अम्भज)

Meaning/ Scientific term: Lotus

Description: See Abja

Reference: Raghu – 10.69, Kumāra – 12.23

Ambu (अम्बु)

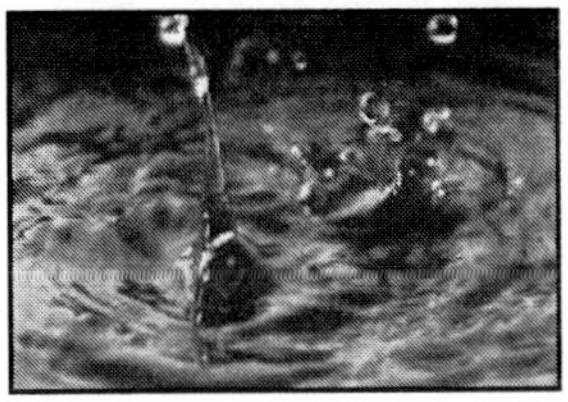

Meaning/ Scientific term: Water (H_2O)

Description: See Ambha

Reference: Raghu – 3.53, 9.82, 13.2, 13.6. 16.65, 17.60, 19.9, Mālā 3.17, Vik - 4, Abhi - 5.12, Ṛtu - 3.15, 6.7, Kumāra - 11.25, 14.13

Ambuda (अम्बुद)

Meaning/ Scientific term: Cloud

Description: *See* Ambadhara

Reference: Raghu - 11.79, Ṛtu - 2.16

Ambudha (अम्बुध)

Meaning/ Scientific term: Cloud

Description: A Sea generally refers to a large body of Salt water, but the term is used in other contexts as well. Most commonly, the term refers to a large expanse of Saline water connected with an ocean, and is commonly used as a synonym for ocean. It is also used sometimes to describe a large Saline take that lacks a natural outlet, such as the Caspian Sea.

Reference: Raghu – 12.70

Ambudhara (अम्वुधर)

Meaning/ Scientific term: Cloud

Description: *See* Ambhasa

Reference: Raghu – 6.44

Āmrakut/Āmra (आम्रकुट)

Meaning/ Scientific term: Mango; Mango Tree (*Mangifera indica*)

Description: Mango is fruit that belongs to the genus mangifera, consisting of numerous pecuious of tropical fruiting trees in the flowering plants families' Ancardiaceae of which Mangifera indica or the common mango is commonly cultivated and indigeneous to the Indian subcontinent. The mango is cultivated in many tropical and sub-tropical reasons and distributed widely in the world. Mango is one of the most extensively exploited fruits for food, juice, flavour, fragrants and colour. It is the national food of India, Pakistan and the Philippines. Mango blossoms are also used in the worship of the Goddess Saraswati. Mango leaves are used to decorate archways and doors in Indian houses during weddings and celebrations like Ganesh Chaturthi, Durgapajā, Paus Saṁkrānti etc.

Reference: Megha - 17, 18, Ṛtu - 6.28, 23, Abhi - 5, Kumāra - 8.78, Nalo-2.13

Aṃśu (अंशु)

Meaning/ Scientific term: Moon

Description: The moon is the Earth's only natural satellite and the fifth largest satellite in the solar system. The average distance (centre to centre) from the Earth to the Moon is 3,84,403 km. which is about thirty times the diameter of the Earth. The Moon makes a complete orbit around the Earth every 27.3 days (the orbital period), and the periodic variations in the geometry of the Earth-Moon-Sun system are responsible for the phases of the Moon, which repeat every 29.5 days (the synodic period). The pull of gravity at its surface is about 17 percent less of that at the Earth's surface. The Moon is the only celestial body on which human beings have made a manned landing.

Reference: Raghu - 6.66 15.10, 19.8, Ṛtu 6.28, Nalo - 2.48

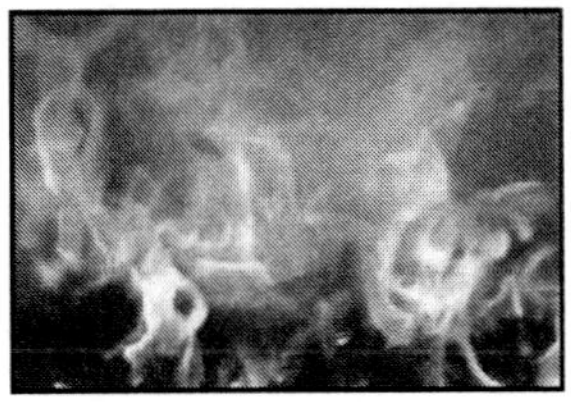

Anal (अनल)

Meaning/ Scientific term: Fire

Description: See Agni

Reference: Śrngāra - 1, Nalo - 4.23

Anḍaja (अन्डज)

Meaning/ Scientific term: Egg originated

Description: In most birds, reptiles, insects, fish after fertilization the resultant all becomes a Zygote. To enable incubation the egg is usually kept within a favourable temperature range as it nourishes and ponfeets the growing embryo. When the embryo is adequately developed it breaks out of the egg in the process of hatching.

Reference: Ṛtu - 3.3. 3.14

Andhakāra (अन्धकार)

Meaning/ Scientific term: Darkness

Description: Darkness is the absence of light, also called lightlessness. A dark object reflects all the light photons than other objects, and therefore appears dim in comiparisa.

Reference: Raghu - 7.42 Vik - 4, Abhi - 6. Nalo -2.49

Angāra (अंगार)

Meaning/ Scientific term: Coal

Description: Coal is readily combustible black or dark brownish sedimentary rock normally occurring in rock strata in layers or veins called coal beds. The harder form, such. as zanthracite coal can be regarded as metamorphic rock because of later exposure to elevated temperature and pressure. Coal is fossill fuel, non-renewable source of our energy, generation of electricity world wide.

Reference: Raghu - 7.43, Puspavanavilasa 9.12, 14

Anila (अनिल)

Meaning/ Scientific term: Air

Description: Air is the mixture of gases comprising the Earth's atmosphere. The mixture contains a group of gases of nearly constant concentrations and a group with concentrations that are variable in both space and time. The atmosphere gases of steady concentration (and their proportions in percentage by volume) are as follows: Nitrogen (N2) 78.084, Oxygen (O_2) 20.946, Argon (Ar) 0.934, Neon (Ne) 0.0018, Helium (He) 0.000524, Methane (CH_4) 0.0002, Krypton (Kr) 0.00014, Hydrogen (H_2) 0.00005, Nitrous Oxide (N,O) 0.00005, Xenon (Xe) 0.0000087. Besides this the typical concentrations ranges of some other gases (in % by volume) are, Water vapour (H_2O) 0 to 7, Carbon dioxide (CO_2) 0.01 to 0.1, Ozone (03) 0 to 0.01, Sulfer dioxide (SO_2) 0 to 0.0001, nitrogens dioxide (NO_2) 0 to 0.00002. Although present in relative's small amounts, these variable constitutant's may be very important for maintaing life on Earth's surface. Water vapour is the source for all forms of precipitation and is an important absorber and emitter of infrared radiation. Carbon dioxide, besides being involved in the process of photosynthesis, is also an important absorber of infrared radiation. Ozone, which is present mainly in the atmospheric region 10 to 50 km. (6 to 30 miles) above the Earth's surface, is an effective absorber of ultraviolet radiation from the Sun and effectively shilds Earth from all radiations of wavelengths less than 3,000 angstroms.

Reference: Raghu - 9.68, 14.54, 16.25, 19.15, Abhi - 7.12, Ṛtu - 6.22, Nalo - 2.37, Puspavanavilasa -8

Anjana (अन्जन)

Meaning/ Scientific term: Collyrium

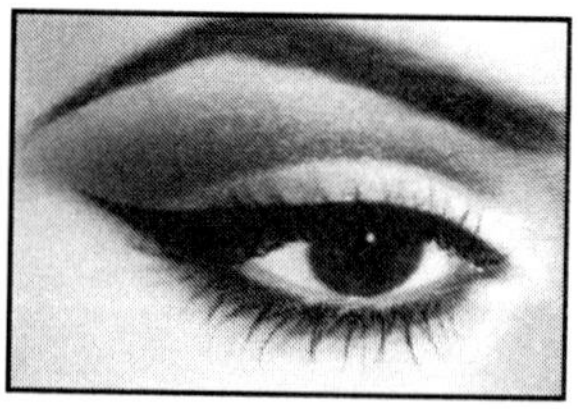

Description: In eye care, a collyrium is a lotion or liquid wash used as a cleaner for the eyes; particularly in diseases of eye. The word collyrium comes from the Greek, ey-salve.

Reference: Raghu - 8.35, 19.10, Mālā 3.5. Ṛtu - 1.11, 2.2, 3.5, 4.17, Śṛngāratilakam - 3, Puśpavānavilasa - 14, 15

Ankur (अंकुर)

Meaning/ Scientific term: Sapling

Description: A young tree with a trunk less than 4 inches (10 cm.) in diameter at a point approximately 4 feet (1.2 m.) above the ground.

Reference: Raghu - 9.43, 16.18, Vik - 2.6, 3.12, Abhi - 2.13, 6.3, Ṛtu - 2.5, 2.8, Śruto - 32, Śrngāraṣṭakam – 4

Ankuś (अंकुश)

Meaning/ Scientific term: Iron rod

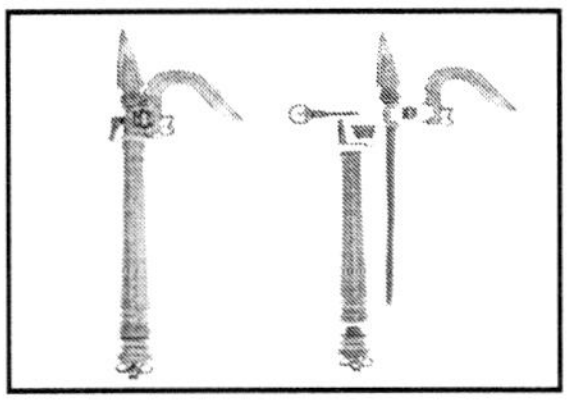

Description: Ankuś is an accountrement employed in the handling and training of elephants. It consists of a hook (usually bronze or steel) which is attached to a two-or three- foot handle that may be constituted of metal, ivory or wood. The hook is inserted into the elephant's sensitive skin, either slightly or more deeply, to cause pain and induce the elephant to belive in a certain manner.

An Ankuś, a sharpened goats with a pointed hook, was the main tool for managing an elephant. The ankuś first appeared in India in the 6th-5th century BC and has been used ever since, not only there, but wherever elephants served man.

Reference: Raghu - 4.39, 15.97, 16.16. 16.81

Anśuk (अंशुक)

Meaning/ Scientific term: Silk, Silk cloth

Description: Silk is a substance produced by silkworms which is made into smooth fine cloth. We can also refer to this cloth or thread as silk. Silk is a natural protein fibre, some forms of which can be woven into textiles. The best-known type of Silk is obtained from the cocoons of the larvae of the mulberry silkworm *Bombyx mori* reared in captivity. The Shimmering appearance of silk is due to the triangular prism-like structure of the silk fibre which allows Silk cloth to refract incoming light at different angles thus producing different colors. Silks are produced by several other insects, but only the silk of moth caterpillars has been used for textile manufacturing. There has been some research into other silks, which differ at the molecular level. Silks are mainly produced by the larvae of insects undergoing complete metamorphosis, but also by some adult insects such as webspinners. Silk production is especially common in the Hymenoptera (bees, wasps, and ants), and is sometimes used in nest construction. Silk is a protain fibre, secreted from silk gland of silkworms and some other insects.

India (14%) is the second largest producer of Silk after China (54%). To produce 1kg of silk, 104 kg of mulberry leaves must be eaten by 3000 silkworms. It takes about 5000 silkworms to make a pure silk kimono. A majority of the silk in India is produced in

Karnataka State. India is also the largest consumer of Silk in the world. Silk is worn by people as a symbol of royalty while attending functions and during festivals. Historically silk was used by the upper classes, while cotton was used by the poorer classes. Today silk is mainly produced in Bhoodhan Pochampally (also known as Silk City), Kanchipuram, Dharmavaram, Mysore, etc. "Murshidabad silk", famous from historical times, is mainly produced in Malda and Murshidabad district of West Bengal and woven with hand looms in Birbhum and Murshidabad district. In the northeastern State of Assam, three different types of silk are produced, collectively called Assam silk: Muga, Eri and Pat silk. Muga, the golden silk, and Eri are produced by silkworms that are native only to Assam. As the process of harvesting the silk from the cocoon kills the larvae, sericulture has been criticized in the early 21st century by animal rights activists, especially since artificial silks are available. Mahatma Gandhi was also critical of silk production based on the Ahiṁsā philosophy "not to hurt any living thing." This led to Gandhi's promotion of cotton spinning machines, an example of which can be seen at the Gandhi Institute. He also promoted Ahimsa silk, wild silk made from the cocoons of wild and semi-wild silk moths. Ahiṁsā silk is promoted in parts of Southern India for those who prefer not to wear silk produced by killing silkworms.

Reference: Raghu 9.43, Vik - 5.12, Ṛtu - 4.3, 4.16, 6.4, 19

Anyabhṛta (अन्यर्भित)

Meaning/ Scientific term: Cuckoo

Description: *See* Anyapuṣṭa

Reference: Mālā - 1, 4, 2, 5.1, Vik - 1.3, 4, Ṛtu - 6.22, 28, Ṛtu - 2.16, Raghu - 9.43, 9.47, Kumāra - 1.45, Raghu - 8.59, 9.34

Anyapuṣṭa (अन्यपुष्ट)

Meaning/ Scientific term: Cuckoo/Indian Cuckoo - *Cuculus micropterus* Family Cuculidae

Description: A Cuckoo is a bird that has a call of two quickotes and lays Cuckoo its egg in other birds nest.

Reference: Mālā - 1, 4, 2, 5.1, Vik - 1.3, 4, Abhi - 4.10. 5.22. 6, Ṛtu - 6.22, 28, 2.16. Kumāra - 1.45, Raghu - 8.59, 9.34, 9.43, 47

Araṇya (अरण्य)

Meaning/ Scientific term: Forest

Description: A forest or woodland is a vast area found in nature with a high density of plants and trees. Forest can be found in all regions capable of sustaining tree growth, at altitude up to the tree line, except where natural fire frequency or other disturbance is too high, or where the environment has been altered by human activity. Forests sometimes contain many tree species only within a small area (as in tropical rain forests and temperate deciduous forests), or relatively few species over large areas. *Sundorban* is a typical example of mangrove forest.

Reference: Kumāra - 4.12, Raghu - 10.80, Abhi - 1.30, Ṛtu - 1.22, 1.26, 6.19

Āraṇyaka (आरण्यक)

Meaning/ Scientific term: Forestry

Description: The branch of science or the art or practice of planting, managing and caring for forests and related natural resources. Forestry is the subject which deals with the forest ecosystems. the most important component of the biosphere. Forestry has emerged as a vital field of science, applied art and technology.

Reference: Abhi - 2.13

Aravinda (अरविन्द)

Meaning/ Scientific term: Lotus

Description: *See* Abja

Reference: Kumāra 1.32, 3.56. 9.1, 9.20, 13.12, 13.17. 17.49. Abhi - 3.5, Raghu - 1.43, 3.17, 6.26, 36, 86, 9.80, 10.8, 62, 13.57, 6.13, 13.23, 14.50, 16.16, 17.23, Ṛtu - 4.13, 4.1, 13, 14, 2.14, 3,1, 15, 6.2, 7.5, Megha– 70, Śṛngaratilakam – 7

Arjuna (अर्जुन)

Meaning/ Scientific term: Arjun Tree (*Terminalia arjuna*)

Description: Arjuna is a large evergreen tree (20-25 m tall) with spreading branches and fast growing. Its gray coloured thick bark pale white externally and smooth inside and flakes off in large flat pieces. The leaves are simple, sub-opposite to each other and are oblong or elliptic-oblong in shape. The tree is common throughout the greater part of Indian peninsula along rivers, streams, ravines and dry watercourses. It is basically a tropical species. It grows almost in all types of soils but it prefers humid, fertile loam and red lateritic soils. Arjun tree is recommended for reclamation of waterlogged areas and for social forestry. Arjun is known for its medicinal values in bark as a diuretic and useful for relief in symptomatic hypertension. It is considered to be a reputedcardiac tonic in the Ayurvedic system of medicine. Bark is used in about 12 Ayurvedic preparations. Although flowering and fruiting starts after 6-7 years of planting, bark is removed not before 15 years of growth to get quality product. Only thick bark is cut away. The harvesting is done during dry period before the spring (April - May). The bark is of great economic value as it contains 20-24% tannin and used for tanning and dying. It is used in hypertension, and ulcers, the bark is astringent, cooling, anti dysenteric urinary astringent, anemia and vitiated conditions of pitta. The bark is popularly used as a cardiotonic. The bark is useful in diseases of the heart, allays thirst and relieves fatigue. This is ethno-botanical use as well traditional use.

Reference: Ṛtu - 2.17, 3.13, 17.51, 19.37

Arka (अर्क)

Meaning/ Scientific term: Sun

Description: The Sun is the star at the center of the Solar system. It has a diameter of about 1,392,000 km, about 109 times that of Earth, and its mass (about 2 x 10 kilograms, 330.000 times that of Earth) accounts for about 99.86% of the total mass of the Solar System. About three quarters of the Sun's mass consists of hydrogen, while the rest is mostly helium. Less than 2% consists of heavier elements, including oxygen, carbon, neon, iron, and others. The Sun is only source of all our energy. Renewable source of energy.

Reference: Raghu - 5.35, 12.100, Abhi - 2.9, 4.2, 17.11, Raghu 6.66, 11.24, Ṛtu 3.23

Arṇab (अर्णव)

Meaning/ Scientific term: Sea

Description: *See* Ambudha

Reference: Raghu - 7.54. 9.11. 9.1 10.3, 10.21, 10.26, 10.85, 12.66

Aruṇa (अरुण)

Meaning/ Scientific term: Early morning Sun

Description: The Sun is only source of our energy. It is the star at the centre of the Solar system and itself accounts for about 99.86% of the Solar system's mass. The Sun's mass consists of hydrogen, while most of the rest is helium. Less than 2% consists of other elements, including iron, oxygen, carbon & neon.

Reference: Raghu - 5.71, 5.72, Mālā - 3, 3.5, 5.5, Abhi - 1.29, 4.2. 6.11, Ṛtu - 3.5, 4.6, 6.4. Nalo - 2.30, 2.48, Puspavanavilasa-6 Raghu 7.42. Ṛtu-4.15

Arunāṃśu (अरुणांशु)

Meaning/ Scientific term: Purple glow

Description: A glow is a dull, steady light, for example the light produced by a fire when there are no flames. It something glows, it looks bright because it is reflecting light.

Reference: Raghu - 5.69

Asana (असन)

Meaning/ Scientific term: Tree *(Terminalia elliptica)*

Description: *Synonym - Terminalia tomentosa,* a member of the Combretaceae family, is a large tree found in deciduous forests. As the tree stands bare during winter (November to February), it can only be identified by its scissored and cracked bark and for this reason is sometimes known as crocodile bark tree. Large amounts of water (at least 4 to 6 I) can be collected by making a small hole in the tip of the lateral ridge with the help of a sickle. Although slightly off-flavoured and orange-yellowish in colour (may be due to dissolved phytochemicals), the water is of potable quality. Tribal people do tap the water to quench their summer thirst.

Reference: Raghu - 9.63

Aśoka (अशोक)

Meaning/ Scientific term: Aśoka tree (*Saraca asoca*)

Description: This very handsome, small, erect evergreen tree is native to India subcontinent, especially in India and SriLanka. This plant belongs to the *caesalpiniaceae* subfamily of the legume family. It is a rain-forest tree. The leaves are deep green, pinnate, dropping; the leaflets are 4-6 in pipers i.e. growing in a dense clusters. The young leaves are red in colour. The flowers bloom in January to May. The flowers are very fragrant. The pods are linear - oblong, compressed and 4-8 seeded. The tree is one of the sacred trees in India and is worshiped in Chaitra month of Indian Bengali calendar. The bark of this tree is strong astringent and used in uterine infections.

Mythology and tradition: As an artistic element, often the tree and the Yakshi are subject to heavy stylization, some authors told that the young girl at the foot of this tree is based on and ancient fertility symbol. The aśoka tree has a symbolic importance in Buddhism. Queen Māyā of Sakya is said to have given birth to the Buddha under an Aśoka tree in a garden in Lombini. In Hinduism the Aśoka is considered a shored tree. It is also associated with Kāmadeva, the Hindu god of love, who included and Aśoka blossom among the five flowers in his quiver. Hence, the Aśoka tree is often mentioned in classical Indian religious and quorous poetry, having at least 16 different names in Sanskrit referring to the tree or it flowers. In Mahākāvya, or India epic poetry, the Aśoka tree is mentioned in the Rāmayana in reference to the Aśoka Vātikā (garden of Ashoka tree) where Hanumāna first meets Śitā.

Reference: Megha – 17, Kumāra - 3.53, 26, Raghu - 13.32, 7.21. 8.62, 63, 9.28, Mālā-3, 3.5, 3.17, 4. Nalo - 2.9. Vik - 2.7, 4.34, 4.62, 5.3, Ṛtu - 6.5, 16, Śruto-32

Aśru (अश्रु)

Meaning/ Scientific term: Tear; Tears are a clear liquid secreted by lacrimal gland

Description: Tears are the liquid product of a process of crying to clean and lubricate the eyes. The word 'lacrimation' (from *L. Lacrima* meaning Tear) (also spelled *lachrynation)* may also be used in a medical or literary sense to refer to crying. Strong emotions, such as sorrow or elation, may lead to crying. The process of yandning may also result in lacrimation. Although most land mammals have a lacrimation system to keep their eyes moist.

Reference: Raghu - 8.86, 15.52, 19.22, Abhi - 2, 3.11, 6.15

Aśva (अश्व)

Meaning/ Scientific term: Horse (Hari, Haya, Turaga, Vaha, Vājin) Damesticated horse- *Equus ferus caballus*

Description: The Horse is a hooved mammal, a subspecies of the family Equidae. The Horse has evolved over the past forty five to fifty five million years from a small multitoed creature into the large, single toed animal of today. Humans began to domesticate horses around 4000 B.C. and their domestication is believed to have been wide spread by 3000 B.C.

Reference: Kumāra - 6.39. . I5.15- 15.31, 16.28. 16.43. Raghu- 3.50, 3.65, 4.70, 4.71, 7.39. 7.42. 7.44. 7.47, 7.52, 18.23. Mālā - 5.14. Abhi-I

Aśvakhura (अश्वखुर)

Meaning/ Scientific term: Horse shoe

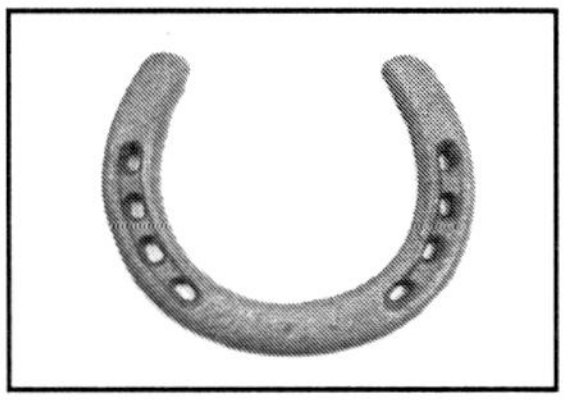

Description: A horseshoe is a piece of metal shaped like a U, which is fixed with nails to the bottom of a horse's foot in order to protect it from decay due to friction.

A horseshoe is an object in the shape of a horseshoe which is used as a symbol of good luck. especially at a hindu marriage or wedding.

Reference: Raghu - 9.50

Ātapa (आतप)

Meaning/ Scientific term: Sun ray (Surya rasmi)

Description: Ray of light comes from the Sun at day time. Through this sun ray, enormous energy (i.e., light energy) comes from the Sun to Earth.

Reference: Raghu - 1.52, 4.5, Vik - 5.16, Abhi - 3, Mālā - 5.3, Abhi - 5.6. Ṛtu 4.16, Śṛngaratilakam - 10

Avayava (Pracamānavayāva) (अवयव)

Meaning/ Scientific term: Shape of a thing or a substance

Description: The shape of an object located in some space is a geometrical description of the part of that space occupied by the object, as determined by its external boundary-abstracting from location and orientation in space, size, and other properties such as colour, content and material composition.

Reference: Raghu - 3.7, 18.49

Ayaskānta (अयसकान्त)

Meaning/ Scientific term: Gem, any previous stone

Description: Precious or semi-precious or jewel is a piece of attractive mineral, which when cut and polished is used to make jewelery or other ornaments. However, certain rocks (such as lapis-lazuli) and organis materials (such as amber) are not minerals, but are still used for jewelery and are therefore often considered to be gemstones as well. Most gemstone is hard, but some soft minerals are used in jewelry because of their luster.

Reference: Kumāra - 2.59, Raghu - 17.63

Āyata, Āyatana (आयत, आयतन)

Meaning/ Scientific term: Volume of a substance

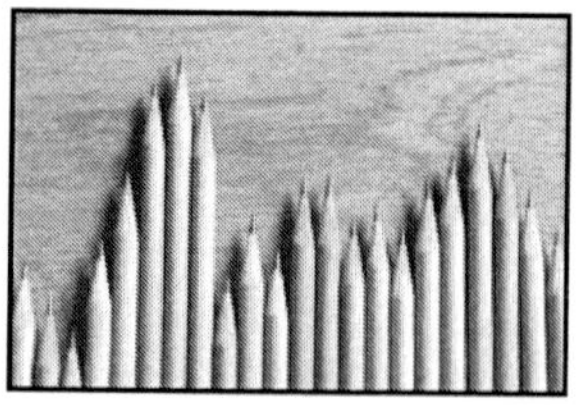

Description: The volume of any solid, liquid, gas or vacuum is how much three-dimensional space it occupies, often quantified numerically one-dimensional figures (such as lines) and two dimensional shapes (such as squares) are assigned zero volume in the three-dimensional space.

Volume is commonly presented in units such as cubic meters, cubic centimeters, liters or mililiters.

Reference: Nalo- 4.9

Āyudha/Astra (आयुध)

Meaning/ Scientific term: Weapon

Description: A weapon is something objects such as a gun, a knife or a missile which is used to kill or hurt people in a fight or war.

Reference: Raghu - 7.4, 7.59, 11.76, 79, 15.88, Abhi - 3, Raghu - 12.51. 12.76, 86, 92, 16.81, Vik-4.11

B

Bakula (बकुल)

Meaning/ Scientific term: Bakula Tree/flower Botanical Name: *Mimusops elengi (Sapotaceae)*

Description: Bakulla tree is an ornamental plant and has white flower with sweet fragrance. The bakula, it is said, blossoms when sprinkled with sweet wine from the mouth of a beautiful woman. An ornamental tree it has fragrant white flowers. Poets fancy that the bakula's flowers owe their sweetness to the wine that the tree is sprinkled with, and it is that draws the bees to them. That and perhaps too the heavy scent they exude. It is a small to large evergreen tree that reaches upto the height of 15m. Bakula flowers are white in color star shaped and pedicellate. Color of stem bark of bakula tree is dark, grey with few crack on the surface. Leaves are variable from oblong to elliptical, glossy and dark green.

Different *Sanskrit* Name:

Bakula – The flower as its flowers are very attractive *Madhugandha-* Means its flowers have very pleasant smell *Chirapushpa-* Means its flowers stay for long time on it *Sthiropushpa-* As its flowers never loss their smell even after drying.

Useful part: Bark, fruit, flowers

Medicinal value: Bakul or Bakula (Mimusops elengi) is an ayurvedic herb that helps in the management of gastric ulcers by decrease gastric acid secretory activity along with strengthening of mucosal defensive mechanisms. *Bakula* possess calcium blocking property so it can be used in management of hypertension. Boil the bakula leaves in water to get excellent mouthwash (Danta dadharyakara) that has the capability of preventing bad or foul breath, dental caries, just like Neem. Regular use of bakula also keeps teeth and gums very strong and in place. Even it has antiseptic and curative properties so can be used on wounds. It is also a cardiac rejuvenator. Bakula is useful in urinary tract infection. Acts as anti-pyretic. Very effective in menstrual problems.

Reference: Raghu - 8.64. 930, 19.12, Ṛtu - 11.24

Bāri/Bāriyantra (वारि)

Meaning/ Scientific term: Water

Description: *See* Ambha

Reference: Raghu - 6.48, 11.5, 16.61, 16.64, 16.66, 17.10, Mālā - 2.12, Vik - 4.3, Ṛtu - 1.1, 2.12. 15, Mālā - 1.6.

Bhānu (भानु)

Meaning/ Scientific term: Sun

Description: *See* Bhāskara

Reference: Raghu - 5.71, Ṛtu - 1.16, 5.2

Bhāskara (भास्कर)

Meaning/ Scientific term: Surya/ Sun

Description: *See* Arka

Reference: Kumāra - 8.29. Raghu 10.74, 11.7, 21, 12.25

Bhasma (भस्म)

Meaning/ Scientific term: Ash

Description: Ash is the 'solid remains' or products of fire of a substanse. *Like cigar ash:* the ash powdered when a cigar is smoked. *Wood ash:* products of wood after combustion. *Volcanic ash:* materials ejected from the top of a volcano. *Fly ash:* products of coal after combustion. In analytical chemistry ash is the compounds that remain after a scientific sample is burned.

Reference: Raghu - 11.86

Bhauma (भौम)

Meaning/ Scientific term: Soil related/originate from soil

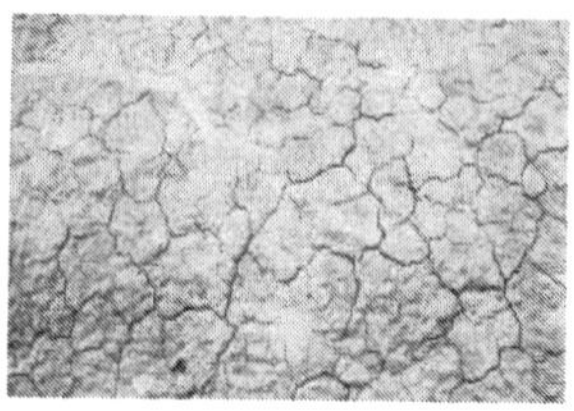

Description: Soil is also known as earth: it is the substance from which our planet takes its name. Little of the soil composition of planet Earth is older than the Tertiary and most no older than the Pleistocene. In engineering, soil is referred to as regolith, or loose rock material. Darkened topsoil and reddish subsoil layers are typical in some regions, Underground water, mineral etc.

Reference: Abhi - 5.4, Raghu - 2.74, 13.18, 14.40, 15.59, 16.55, 84, 18.48, Ṛtu - 3.5, 6.19

Bheka (भेक)

Meaning/ Scientific term: Frog

Description: A frog is a small creature with smooth and/or rough skin, big eyes. Amphibian having long hind legs which are used for jumping, Frogs usually live near water. Frogs are widely known as exceptional jumpers and many of the anatomical characteristics of frogs, particularly their long powerful legs.

Reference: Ṛtu - 2.13

Bhramara/Bhramari (भ्रमर)

Meaning/ Scientific term: Bee

Description: Bees are a monophyletic lineage within the superfamily *Apoidea,* presently classified by the unranked taxa on name *Anthophila.* They are the flying insects closely related to wasps and ants, and are known for their role in pollination and for producing honey and bees wax.

Reference: Nalo - 2.15, 2 16, 2.57

Bhṛngina/Bhṛnga (भृंग)

Meaning/ Scientific term: Bees/Honey Bees

Description: Bees are a monophyletic lineage within the superfamily *Apoidea,* presently classified by the unranked taxaon name *Anthophila.* They are the flying insects closely related to wasps and ants, and are known for their role in pollination and for producing honey and bees wax.

Reference: Ṛtu - 2.14, 6.21, 24

Bhu (भु)

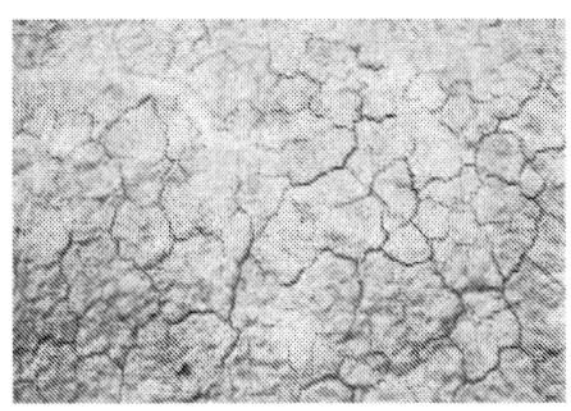

Meaning/ Scientific term: Soil/ Earth

Description: *See* Bhumi/Bhauma

Reference: Abhi - 5, Raghu - 2.74, 13.18, 14.40, 15.59, 16.55, 84, 18.48, Ṛtu - 3.5, 6.19, Nalo - 1.8, 1.51

Bhudhara (भुधर)

Meaning/ Scientific term: Planet Earth

Description: The term earth may merely imply the surface configuration with distinctive form characteristies which can be attributed to the dominance of particular process or particular structures in the course of its development. Earth (or the Earth) is the third planet from the Sun and the densest and fifth-largest of the eight planets in the Solar System. It is also the largest of the Solar System's four terrestrial planets. It is sometimes referred to as the World, the Blue Planet.

Reference: Kumāra - 1.19

Bhujanga (भुजंग)

Meaning/ Scientific term: Snake/Sarpa/Phani *(Elaphe obsoleta/Elapidae/Viperidae)*

Description: Snake are elongate, legless, carnivorous reptiles of the suborder *Serpentes* that can be distinguished from legless lizard by their lack of eyepids and external ears, like all squamats snakes are ectothermic, anoniok vertebrates in overlapping scales. Many species of snakes have skull, with many more joints than their lizard ancestors. enabling them to swallow prey much larges than their heads with their highly mobile jaws.

Symbolism:

India is called the land of snakes. Snakes are worshipped as snake pits (despite snakes' oversion for milk). The Cobra is seen in the neck of Shiva and Vishnu is depicted often as sleeping on a seven-headed snake or within the coils of a serpent. There are also several temples in India solely for cobras sometimes called *Nāgrāj* (King of snakes) and it is believed that snakes are symbols of fertility. There is a Hindu festival called 'Nāg Panchami' each year on which day snakes are venerated and prayed to. In India there is another mythology about snakes. Commonly known in Hindi as Ichchhādhari snakes. Such snakes on take the form of any living creature, but refer human form. These mythical snakes possess a valuable gem called 'Mani', which is more brilliant than diamond.

***Religion*:**

Snakes are part of Hindu worship. Some notable snakes in Hinduism are Ananta Vasuki, Taxak, Karkotaka and Pingla. The term Nāga is used to refer to eatities that take the form of large snakes in Hinduism or Buddhism.

Reference: Raghu - 1.80. 2.74, 13.12, 16.77, 17.63, Vik - 2, 5.18, Mālā - 4, Ṛtu 1.13. 20. 2.13

Bhumi (भुमि)

Meaning/ Scientific term: Soil; surface soil; surface of the earth

Description: The soil covering of the earth's outer shell may be defined as that part of the crust which extends downwards from the surface as deeply as living organisms penetrate.

Reference: Abhi - 5.4, Raghu - 2.74, 13.18, 14.40, 15.59, 16.55, 84, 18.48, Ṛtu - 3.5, 6.19

Bhurjapatra (भुर्जपत्र)

Meaning/ Scientific term: A type of plant leaf (*Betula bhojpatra*) Genus - Betula, Family: Betulaceae

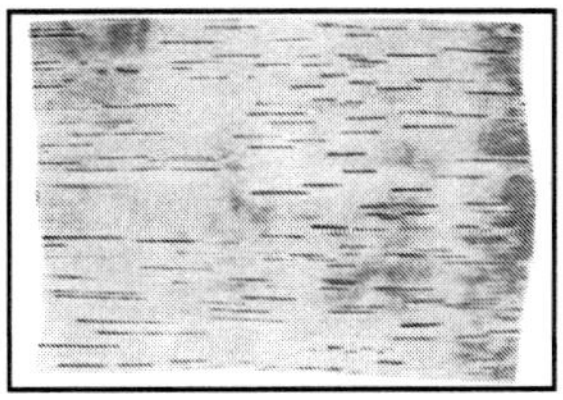

Description: Bhurjapatra was writing material in ancient time in Nothern India. In Kashmir and Himachal Pradesh it was available in plenty. In medieval period people generally used the Bhurjapatra for writing Bijamantras. Bhurjapatra is the inner bark of a tree and leaf as the name might indicate. The Bhurja tree is the Silver birch, botanically identified as *Betula utilis* or *Betula bhojpatra* which is very commonly grown in the Himalayan slopes (above 30,000 feet high) only (from Kashmir to Sikim). Alberuni calls the tree tuz It is also called 'Lekhan'. The other uses of this bark are roofing houses, warpping things. etc. It is popular in North India but not so in South. because of its paucity.

According to the Greek historians this was very popular in India as writing matcrial. The oldest Bhurja patra manuscript known so far belongs to the 2nd or 3rd century AD. It is found in fragments that described Dhammapada written with Kharosti script. The use of Bhurja patra as writing material continued upto the Mughal period. Later, paper replaced both palm leaf and Bhurja patra. However, Bhurja patra, which is supposed to be very sacred writing material in India, is used till today for writing religious books as well as for preparing sacred mantras. The inner bark of bhurja tree was the most popular material for writing manuscripts, especially in north east - western India. AI-Birumi informs 'in central and northern India people use the bark of the fur tree. One kind of which is used as a cover for sows. It is called bhurja. They take a price, one year long, and as broad as the outstretched fingers up the hand, or somewhat loss, and prepare it in various ways. They oil and positively, so as to make it hard and smooth and they write on it.'

Reference: Kumāra - 1.7, 55, 18.14, 19, 19.1, 3, Raghu - 4.73, Vik - 2, Megha - 36

Bhuvana (भुवन)

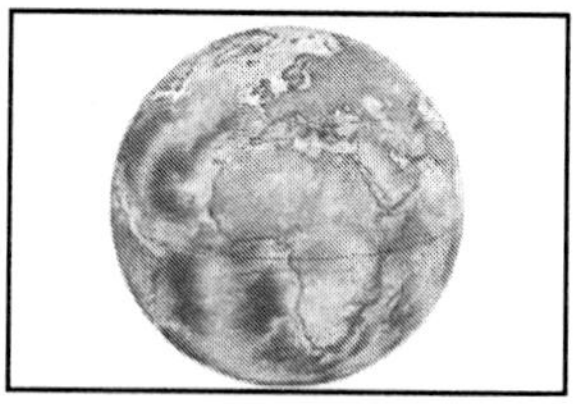

Meaning/ Scientific term: Earth

Description: *See* Bhudhara

Reference: Abhi - 7.26, 7.27

Biḍāla (बिड़ाल)

Meaning/ Scientific term: Cat (*Felis catus*)

Description: A Cat is a fury animal that has a long tail and sharp claws. Cats are often kept as pets. Cats are with lions, tigers and other wild animals placed in the same family. Cats have been associated with humans for long times and are currently the most popular pet in the world.

Reference: Abhi - 6, Mālā - 4

Bīja (बीज)

Meaning/ Scientific term: Seed

Description: A seed is a small embryonic plant enclosed in a covering called the seed coat, usually with some stored food. It is the product of the ripened ovule of gymnosperm and angiosperms plants which occurs after fertilization and some growth within the mother plant.

Reference: Raghu - 14.77, Abhi - 6.24

Bimāna (विमान)

Meaning/ Scientific term: Aeroplane

Description: A fixed-wing aircraft typically called an airplane. aeroplane or just plane is an aircraft capable of flight using forward motion that generates lift as the using moves through the air. Planes include jet engine and propeller drive vehicles propelled forward by thrust, as well as unpowered aircraft (such as gliders), which use thermals, or warm-air pockets to inherit lift.

Reference: Raghu - 6.1, 7.51, 13.1, 17, 19, 13.44, 68, 76, 14.20, 17.9, Nalo - 2.47, Megha - 63

Bimbaphala (बिम्वफल)

Meaning/ Scientific term: *Momordica monadelpha*

Description: A plant bearing a bright red gourd *Momordica* (Cucurbitaceae)

Synomym: Calpidosicyos, Dimorphoclamys, Eulenburgia, Muricia, Neurosperma, Neurospermum, Nevrosperma, Raphanistrocarpus, Raphanocarpus, Zucca, Balsam Apple, Balsam Pear, Bitter Melon

Reference: Megha - 83, Kumāra - 3.67, Ragau - 13.16, Mālā - 3.5, 4.14

Bṛṣṭi (वृष्टि)

Meaning/ Scientific term: Rain

Description: In scientific term rain is liquid precipitation, as opposed to other kinds of precipitation such as snow, hail and sleet. Rain requires the presence of a thick layer of the atmosphere to have temperatures above the melting point of water near and above the Earth's surface. Two processes possibly acting together can lead to air becoming saturated leading to rainfall cooling the air or adding water vapour to the air. Precipitation forms via collision with rain drops or ice crystals within a cloud. Rain drops range in size from oblate, puncake - like shapes for large drops, to small spheres for smaller drops.

Reference: Raghu - 9.6, 11.91, 12.29, 12.94, 15.25, 17.16, 18.2, Mālā - 4, Megha (Purva) - 20

C

Candana/Candadruma (चन्दन / चन्दद्रुम)

Meaning/ Scientific term: Sandal; sandalwood tree; Indian sandalwood *Santalum album*, synonym = *Sirium myrtifolium*

Description: Sandalwood is the name of different fragrant wood. These woods are yielded by trees in the genes santalum, which are often used for the essential oil of contains. The wood is heavy and yellow in colour as well as fine-graused, and unlike many other aromatic wood's retains its fragrance for decades. Sandalwood has been valued and treasured for many years for its fragrance, carving, medical and religious qualities.

Reference: Raghu - 17.24, Ṛtu - 1.4, 1.6, 1.8, 2.21, 5.3, 6.6, 6.12, Kumāra - 8.25, Śṛngārtilakam 3.26, Puspavānavilāsa 1, Raghu - 4.48, 4.51, 8.71, 10.42, 116.3, 17.24

Candra/Candrikā/Candra Pāda (चन्द्र / चन्द्रिका)

Meaning/ Scientific term: Moon

Description: *See* Aṁśu

Brief Explanation of the Moon Phases:

The phases of the Moon are caused by the relative positions of the Earth, Sun and Moon. The moon goes around the Earth in 27.3 days, or 27 days 7 hours 43 minutes, on average. This measurement is relative to the stars and is called the sidereal period or orbital period. However, because of the Earth's motion around the sun, a complete moon cycle (New Moon to New Moon) appears to earthbound observers to take a couple of days longer: 29.5305882 days to be exact. This number is called the synodic period or 'lunation' and is relative to the sun.

The sun always illuminates the half of the moon facing the sun (except during lunar eclipses, when the moon passes through the earth's shadow. When the sun and moon are on opposite sides of the earth, the moon appears 'full' to us, a bright, round disk. When the moon is between the earth and the sun, it appears dark, a 'new' moon. In between, the Moon's illuminated surface appears to grow (wax) to full, then decreases (wanes) to the next new moon. The edge of the shadow (the terminator) is always curved, being an oblique view of a circle, giving the moon its familiar crescent shape.

Reference: Raghu - 12.36, 79, 96, 13.40, 30, 15.90, 16.18, 17.30, 19.18, 17.30, 19.48, Megha - 9, Ṛtu - 1.28, 3.9, 17, 18, Mālā - 4, 5.7, Vik - 1.12, 3, 3.16, 4.19, 5.11, Ṛtu 3.21, 23, 5.3, Śrngaraṣṭakam - 2. 3, Puspavānavilāsa - 11. 21

Candrakānta (चन्द्रकान्त)

Meaning/ Scientific term: Jewel

Description: A Jewel is a precious stone used to decorate valuable rings that you wear, such as rings or necklace.

Reference: Vik - 5.11, Megha - 9

Candramā (चन्द्रमा)

Meaning/ Scientific term: Moon ray

Description: A Moon ray is a ray of light comes from the Moon at night.

Reference: Raghu - 1.46, 6.22, 8.42, Abhi - 6.18, Ṛtu - 1.9

Cātak (चातक)

Meaning/ Scientific term: A bird of the rainy season. *Clamator jacobinus*

Description: The first Pied Crested Cuckoo, the official harbinger of the south-west monsoon since the days of poet, Kālidāsa. The Pied Crested Cuckoo, also known as Chatak in Kālidāsa's literary work Meghdut has always heralded the advent of rains.

The Jacobin Cuckoo, Pied Cuckoo or Pied Crested Cuckoo is a member of the Cuckoo order of birds that is found in Africa and Asia. It is partially migratory and in India, it has been considered a harbinger of the monsoon rains due to the timing of its arrival. It has been associated with a bird in Indian mythology and poetry, known as the 'Chatak' and represented as a bird with a beak on its heads that waits for rains to quench its thirst. This medium sized, slim black and white cuckoo with a crest is distinctive. The white wins patch on the black wing pattern make it unmistakable even in flight. They are vocal during the breeding season. The species is distributed south of Sahara in Africa and South of the Himalayas in India. Also found in Sri Lanka and Myanmar. This species is widely mentioned in ancient Indian poetry as the chatak. According to Indian mythology it has a beak atop its head and it thirsts for the rains. The poet Kālidāsa used it in his 'Meghadoota' as a metaphor for deep yearning and this tradition continues in literary works in Hindi.

Reference: Kumāra - 6.27, Raghu - 5.17, 17.60, Ṛtu - 2.3, Megha - 9

Chavi (छवि)

Meaning/ Scientific term: Picture, an imitative representation of an object on a surface.

Description: *See* Citra

Reference: Raghu - 11.15, Abhi - 3.8

Chāyā (छाया)

Meaning/ Scientific term: Shadow

Description: A shadow is an area where direct light from light sources cannot reach due to obstruction by a object. It occupies all of the space behind an opaque object with light infront of it. The cross-section of a shadow is a two-dimensional silhouetle, or reverse projection of the object blocking the light. Shadow length changes dramatically throughout the day.

Reference: Raghu - 4.79, 84, 11.11, 13.2, 13.57, 14.40, 16.6, 17.26, 19.28, Vik - 5.8, Abhi - 1, 2.6, 4, 4.11, 5.7, 7.32, Śṛngaraṣṭakam - 5, Puspasvānavilāsa - 16

Chetnā (चेतना)

Meaning/ Scientific term: Consciousness

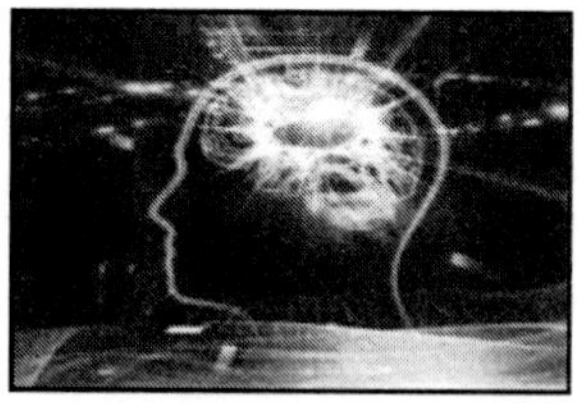

Description: Consciousness is a quality of the mind generally regarded to comprise such key features as subjectivity, self-awareness, sentience, sapience, and the ability to perceive the relationship between oneself and one's environment. It is a subject of much research in philosophy of mind, psychology, neurology, and cognitive science. Some philosophers divide consciousness into *phenomenal consciousness*, which is experience itself, and access consciousness, which is the processing of the things in experience. Some philosophers suggest that consciousness resists or even defies definition. Others believe it can be usefully distinguished between *phenomenal consciousness* and access or *psychological consciousness*, while still others disagree. There are many philosophical stances on consciousness, including: behaviorism, dualism, idealism, functionalism, phenomenalism, physicalism, emergentism, and mysticism. This archive will investigate the nature of consciousness, different levels of consciousness, cosmic consciousness, collective consciousness and spirituality and consciousness. But the ultimate questions is whether consciousness can be permanently altered and the nature of enlightenment. Consciousness is a term with a very wide range of interpretations. However commonly referred meanings allude to perceptual consciousness, and introspective consciousness. Introspective consciousness seems so special because it gives inner awareness of self, and memory of other mental events. Also includes perceiving one's own perceptions with attributes (like good, bad, positive etc.). Normally associated to 'animated matter' and all forms exhibiting 'life'.

Reference: Raghu - 17.1

Chikitshā (चिकित्सा)

Meaning/ Scientific term: Treatment

Description: Treatment is medical attention given to a sick or ill or injured person or animal.

Reference: Mālā - 4

Cinha (चिन्ह)

Meaning/ Scientific term: Sign/Mark

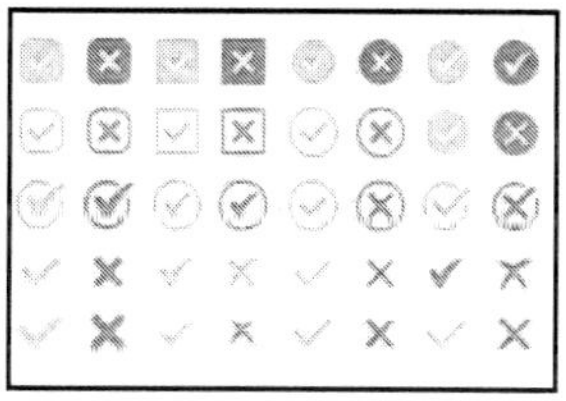

Description: It there is a sign of something, there is something which shows that it exists of is happening. A sign is a mark or shape that always has a particular meaning, for example in mathematics or music.

A sign is a nicc of wood, metal, or plastic with words or pictures on it. Signs give you information about something, or give you a warning or an instruction.

Reference: Raghu- 17.25

Citra/Citrasālā/Citraphalak (चित्र / चित्रशाला)

Meaning/ Scientific term: Picture

Description: A representation of anything (as a person, a flower, a landscape, a building) upon canvas, paper, or other surface, produced by means of painting, drawing, engraving, photography etc.

Reference: Raghu - 5.33, Mālā (Viskambhaka) - 4, Vik - 1, 2, 4.43, Abhi - 4, 6, 6.14, 16, 7, Puṣpa - 18, Raghu - 1.36,2.31, Mālā - 2.2, Abhi - 2.16, Sṛngāratilakm - 22

Curni (चुर्नि)

Meaning/ Scientific term: Dust

Description: Dust is a general name for minute solid particles with diameters less than 500 micrometers.

Reference: Vik - 1.5

Cūta (चुत)

Meaning/ Scientific term: Mango tree (*Mangifera indica*)

Description: *See* Āmrakut / Āmra

Reference: Vik - 2.7, Abhi - 4.13, 5.1, 6.4, 8, Kumāra - 1.27, 2.64, 3.27, 30, 32, 4.14, 38, Raghu - 7.21, 13.34, 19.43, Mālā - 3.4, 4.2, Ṛtu - 6.1, 3, 14, 15, 30

D

Dahana/Dāha/Dāhaśakti/Dagdha (दहन / दाह)

Meaning/ Scientific term: Burning/Power of Burning

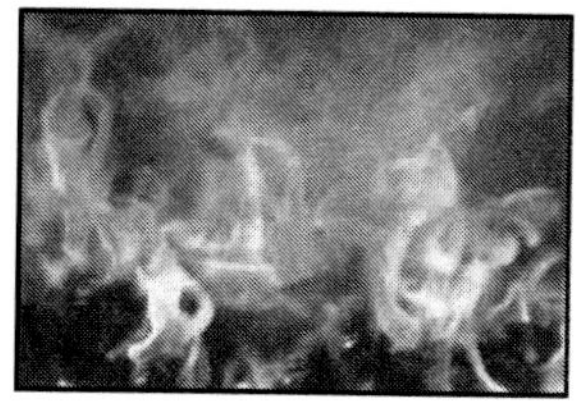

Description: It is the sequence of exothermic chemical reactions between a fuel and an oxidant accompanied by the production of heat and conversion of chemical species. There large of heat can result in the production of light in the form of others glowing or a flame.

Reference: Raghu - 8.20, 11.69, Ṛtu - 6.20, Raghu - 11.42, Mālā - 3.11, 4.4, Abhi - 2.7, 4.4, 6.9, Sṛngāratilakam - 10

Dantina/Dvipa (दन्तिन)

Meaning/ Scientific term: Elephant (Indian elephant *Elephas maximus indicus*)

Description: Elephant are large land mammals having two genera of purely Elephantidae: Elephas and Loxodonta. Three species of elephant are living today – the African Bush Elephant, African Forest Elephant and Asian Elephant (i.e. Indian Elephant). Elephant are the largest land animals now living.

Reference: Raghu - 1.71, Ṛtu - 1.15, 1.16, Kumāra - 8.33, 8.69, 13.25, 13.38, 13.39, 13.41, 14.39, 14.42, 15.8, 15.10, 16.2, 16.28, 16.30, 16.31, 16.32, 16.37, 16.38, 16.50, Nalo - 1.48

Darbha/Durba Grass (दर्भ / दुर्बा)

Meaning/ Scientific term: Grass (*Cynodon dactylon*)

Description: An ayurvedic medicinal grass grown in India. A traditional use of Cynodon is for eye disorders, and weak vision; the afflicted are advised to walk bare foot on dew drops spread over Cynodon plant each morning. Accordingly to Ayurveda, India's traditional pharmacopoeia, Cynodon plant is pungent, bitter, fragrant, heating, vulnerary, anthelmintic, antipyretic, alexiteric. Virus-affected discoloured leaves of Cynodon are used for the treatment of liver complaints.

Reference: Raghu - 11.31, 11.39, 14.69, Abhi - 1.7, 3, Raghu - 13.25, 39, 14.69

Darbhāṁkura (दर्भांकुर)

Meaning/ Scientific term: Grass. Ordinary grass (*Panicum dactylon*) see Darbha.

Description: Grasses or 'graminoids' are monocotyledonous, usually herbaceous plants with narrow leaves growing from the base. The tree grasses include cereals, bamboo and the grasses of lawns (turf) and grassland (Savana). They include the 'true grasses', of the *Poaceae* (or Garm'mease) family, as well as the sedges (Cyperaceae) and the rushes (*Jumcaceae*).

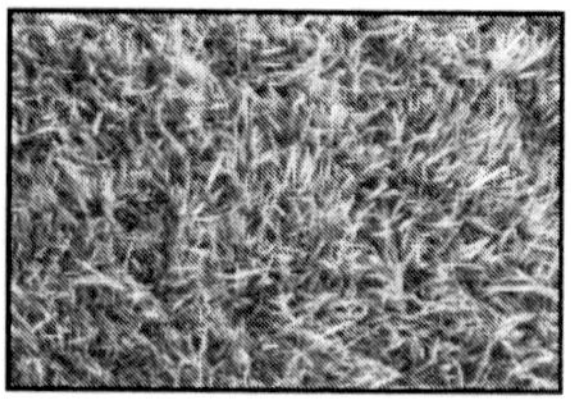

Reference: Raghu - 13.39, Abhi - 4, Kumāra 7.7, 14, Raghu - 6.25, 17.12

Darpana (दर्पन)

Meaning/ Scientific term: Mirror

Description: A mirror is an object with at least one polished and therefore specularly reflective surface. The old fashioned term "looking glass" can be used for personal grooming. The most familiar type of mirror is the plane mirror, which has a flat surface. Curved mirrors are also used, to produce, magnified or diminished images or focus light or simply distant the reflected image.

Reference: Raghu - 10.10, 14.37, 19.28, 30, Abhi - 7.32, Ṛtu - 4.13

Dāva (दाव)

Meaning/ Scientific term: Forestry

Description: The branch of science or the art or practice of planting, managing and caring for forsts and related natural resources. The main goal of forestry is to create and implement system that allow forests to continue a sustainable continuation of currion mental supplies and services. Forestry is the subject which deals with the forest ecosystems, the most important component of the biosphere. Forestry has emerged as a vital field of science, applied art and technology.

Reference: Nalo - 3.17

Dāvam (दावम्)

Meaning/ Scientific term: Forest

Description: A forest or woodland is a vast area found in nature with a high density of plants and trees. Forest can be found in all regions capable of sustaining tree growth, at altitudes up to the tree line, except where natural fire frequency or other disturbance is too high, or where the environment has been altered by human activity. Forests sometimes contain many tree species only within a small area (as in tropical rain forests and temperate deciduous forests), or relatively few species over large areas.

Reference: Raghu - 2.8

Devadāru (देवदारु)

Meaning/ Scientific term: Himalayan Cedar, Biological Name : (*Cedrus deodara Coniferae*)

Description: Badra daru, Deodar, Devadaru, Devataram, Devdari, Pahari-keli, Pinus Deodara, Snehaviddha, Suradaru, Toon, Toona, Toon-maram, Vrikaṣhapa.

Description: This herb is found all over the Northern Himalayas. It is largely cultivated in India as an ornamental tree.

Parts Used: Leaves, wood, bark, turpentine Constituents.

Medicinal Applications: Wood-carminative; Bark-powerfull astringent, febrifuge; Leaves-mild turpentine properties. Cedarwood oil, extracted from the herb, is used for catarrhal conditions of the respiratory tract. It is an expectorant.

Uses: Diarrhea, dysentery, fever, inflammation, kidney stones, paralysis, skin diseases, ulcers. Bark of the herb is a good remedy in remittent and intermittent fevers, diarrhea and dysentery. The powder-is used in the treatment of ulcers. It is particularly valuable for the treatment of bilious fevers and inveterate diarrhea arising from atony of the muscular fiber. Cedarwood oil, extracted from the herb. This is used for catarrhal conditions of the respiratory tract. It is an expectorant. It is also useful for ulcers and skin diseases.

Reference: Megha (uttar) - 46, Kumāra - 1.15, 1.54, 6.51, Raghu - 2.36, 56, 4.76

Dhartri (धरित्रि)

Meaning/ Scientific term: Earth

Description: *See* Bhudhara

Reference: Kumāra - 1.2, 1.17, Abhi - 2.15

Dhātu (धातु)

Meaning/ Scientific term: Metal

Description: A metal is a chemical element that is a good conductor of both electricity and heat and forms ionic bonds with non-metals. In chemistry, a metal is an element, compound, or alloy characterized by high electrical conductivity. In a metal, atoms readily lose electrons to form positive ions (cations). Those ions are surrounded by delocalized electrons, which are responsible for the conductivity. Metals are usually inclined to form cations through electron loss, reacting with oxygen in the air to form oxides over changing time scales (iron rusts over years, while potassium or sodium burns in few seconds). The transition metals (such as iron, copper, zinc, and nickel) take much longer to oxidise, others, like paradium, platinum and gold, do not react with atmosphere at all.

Physical properties: Metals in general have high electrical conductivity, thermal conductivity, luster and the ability to be deformed under stress without cleaving. Optically speaking, metals are opaque, shiny and lustrous.

Mechanical properties: Mechanical properties of metals include ductilily which is largely due to their inherent capacity for plastic deformation. Forces larger than the elastic limit, or heat, may cause a permanent (irreversible) deformation of the object.

Reference: Raghu - 2.29, 3.21, 4.71, 12.58, 15.9, 16.32, Abhi - 2.9

Dhāturasa (धातुरस)

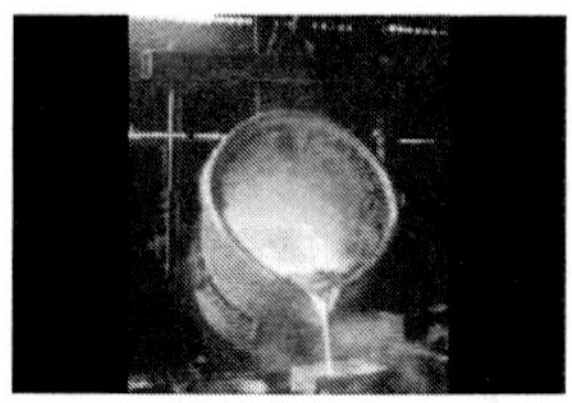

Meaning/ Scientific term: Molten metal

Description: Liquid metal seen by a red coloured soil.

Reference: Kumāra - 1.7, 8.26

Dhuma/Dhumra (धुम / धुम्र)

Meaning/ Scientific term: Smoke

Description: Smoke- is a colloid and comprises a collection of airborne solid and liquid participates and gases emitted when a material undergoes combustion or pyrolysis, together with the quantity of air that is entrained or otherwise mixed into the mass. It is commonly an unwanted by-product of fires (including stoves, candles, oil lamps, and fireplaces), but may also be used for pest control (cf. fumigation), communication (smoke signals), defensive and offensive capabilities in the military (smoke-screen), cooking (smoked salmon), or smoking (tobacco, marijuana, etc.). Smoke is used in rituals, when incense, sage, or resin is burned to produce a smell for spiritual purposes. Smoke is sometimes used as a flavoring agent, and preservative for various foodstuffs. It is commonly an unwanted by-product of fires but may also used for pest control, communication, defense or smoking.

Reference: Raghu - 7.26, 7.27, 7.55, 11.81, 13.29, 13.37, 15.16, 15.49, 15.50, 17.34, Abhi - 4

Dhumaketu (धुमकेतु)

Meaning/ Scientific term: Comet

Description: A comet is a small system body bigger than a meteoroid that when dose enough to the sun, exhibits a visible coma i.e., fuzzy atmosphere and sometimes a tail, both because of the effects of solar radiation upon the comets. Comet nuclei are loose collections of ice, dust and small rocky panicles, ranging from four hundred metres across. The word comet came to the English language through the Latin Cometes from the Greek word Kume, which means "hair of the head". Aristotle first used the derivation Kometes to depict comets as "stars with hair". The astronomical symbol for comets accordingly consists of a disc with a hairlike tail.

Reference: Kumāra - 2.32, Raghu - 11.81

Dhvani (ध्वनि)

Meaning/ Scientific term: Sound

Description: In physics, sound evolved when vibrations which travel through air or water and sensed by the human and, or animal ear. The quality of sound i.e. loud sound.

Reference: Raghu - 4.73, 9.52, 71, 16.13, 87

Dhvani (ध्वनि)

Meaning/ Scientific term: Voice/sound

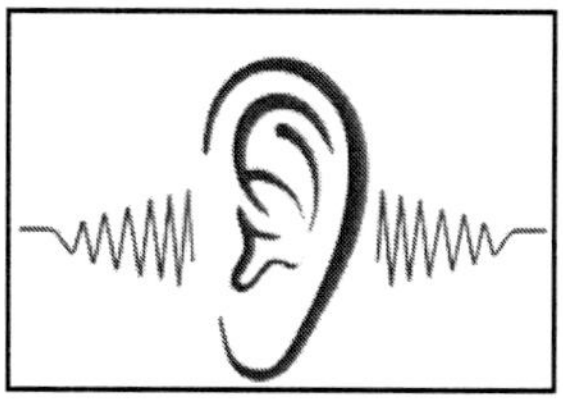

Description: Sound is energy that travels in waves through air, water, or other substance, and can be heard. The sound on a television, radio, or CD/DVD player is what we hear coming from the machine by which its loudness can be controlled.

Reference: Raghu - 9.52, 71, 16.13, 87, Nalo - 3.23, Puṣpa - 21

Drākṣā (द्राक्षा)

Meaning/ Scientific term: Vine creeper (vitis viṁfera)

Description: A vine is a plant that grows up or over things, especially one which produces grapes. A woody climbing plant.

Reference: Raghu - 4.65

Dravina (द्रविन)

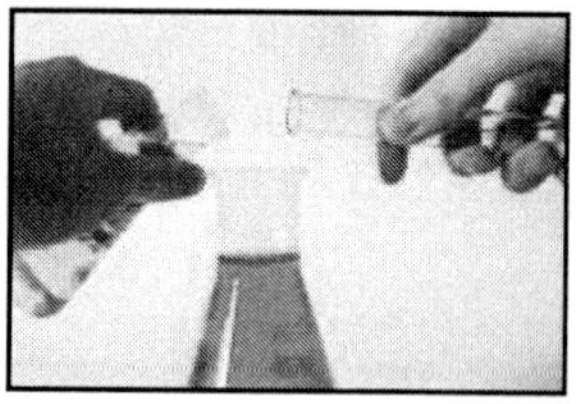

Meaning/ Scientific term: Solution

Description: In chemistry, a solution is a hard geneous mixture composed of two or more substances. In such a mixture, a solute is dissolved in another substance, known a solvent.

Reference: Raghu - 18.14

Druma/Dāru (द्रुम / दारु)

Meaning/ Scientific term: Tree

Description: A tree is a perennial woody plant. It is most often defined as woody plant that has many secondary branches supported clear of the ground on a single main stem or trunk with clear apical dominance. A tree is a plant forms that occur in many different orders and families of plants. Trees show a varity of growth forms, leaf type and shape, bark characterises and reproducer organs.

Reference: Raghu - 8.90, 10.49, 11.23, 75, 12.32, 15.19, 17.12, 44, Mālā - 3.11, Vik- 4.13, Abhi - 1.29, 2.12, 6.29, Ṛtu - 1.26, 2.8, 20, 6.2, 3.15, 18, 25

Duṣana (दुषन)

Meaning/ Scientific term: Pollution

Description: It is introduction of contaminants into an environment that causes instability, disorder, harm or discomfort to the ecosystem i.e. physical systems or living organisms into the atmosphere. Pollution can take the form of chemical substance or energy, such as (excess) noise, heat or light. There are several types of pollution such as air pollution, sound pollution, soil pollution, water pollution etc.

Reference: Raghu - 12.46

Dvirephā (द्विरेफ)

Meaning/ Scientific term: The Bumble Bee

Description: Bumble bee is any genus Bombus, in the family Apidae. There are over 250 known species, existing primarily in the Northern Hemisphere. Bumble bees are social insects that are characterized by black and yellow body hairs.

Reference: Raghu - 6.7, 13, Mālā - 3.5, Ṛtu - 3.6, 6.1, 6.14, 17, Śṛngārasṭakam - 6

Dyuti (द्युति)

Meaning/ Scientific term: Scattering of light

Description: It is light that usually at low temp and is thus a form of cold body radiation by chemical reaction, electrical energy, subatomic notions or stress on a crystal. This distinguishes luminescence from light generated by high temperatures.

Reference: Raghu - 8.29, 17.16, Rtu - 6.18, Sṛngārasṭakam - 3,

Puṣpavānavılāsa - 16

E

Elālatā (एलालता)

Meaning/ Scientific term: Cardamomum Plant (2 genera- *Elettaria* & *Amomum*)

Description: This species used to be known as Amomum Cardamomum. The word Cardamom is sometimes used for species of the closely related Genus Amomum which are also members of the Ginger family. The much larger brown and black Cardamom fruits come from these other species. They have coarser taste and aroma. Black Cardamom, *Amomum subulatum*, is the best known of these related species. The Cardamom is native to India and Srilanka where it occurs in the wild. It has been introduced all over tropical Asia where it is cultivated. The fruits are pale Green to Yellow is colour and elongated oval-shape. Each fruit has 3 Chambers failed with small aromatic seeds very long. The fruits and seeds dry to a straw brown colour and are widely used as flavouring agent.

Reference: Raghu - 4.47, 6.64

G

Gagan (गगन)

Meaning/ Scientific term: Sky

Description: *See* Ambara

Reference: Raghu - 9.50, 10.61, Vik - 1.15, Ṛtu - 3.12

Gaṇḍasthali (गन्डस्थलि)

Meaning/ Scientific term: Throat

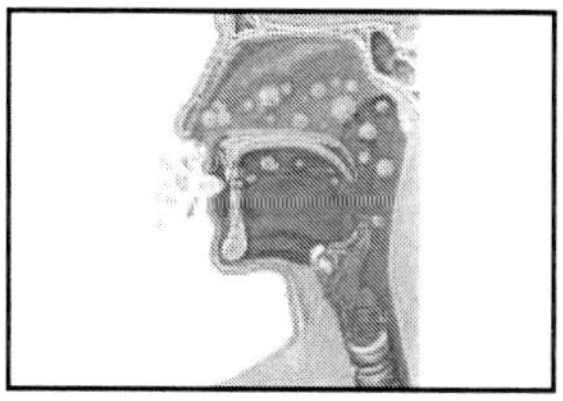

Description: In biology or in anatomy, the throat is the anterior part of the neck, in front of the vertebral column man and woman. It consists of the pharynx and laryax. An important feature of the throat is the epiglottis, a flap which separates the esophagus from the trachea and prevents inhalation of food or drink.

Reference: Raghu - 6.72

Gandha/ghrān (गन्ध / घ्रान)

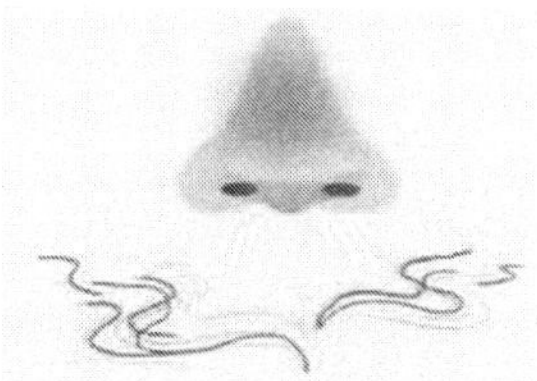

Meaning/ Scientific term: Smell

Description: The sense of smell, the ability of humans and other animals to perceive odors. 'Olfaction' is the sense of smell. Also known as 'olfactkms' or itiore commonly as smell.

Reference: Raghu - 16.87, Abhi - 5.4, Ṛtu - 6.35, 6.36

Gaja (गज)

Meaning/ Scientific term: Elephant

Description: *See* Dantina

Reference: Ṛtu - 1, 15.27, Vik - 4.5, 14, 23, 28, 35, 45, 46, 56, 62, 63, 71, 5.18, Abhi - 1, 7.31, Kumāra - 3.37, 4.31,

7.32, 52, Raghu - 4.29, 45, 69, 76, 5.43, 48, 7.46, 48, 9.10, 15, 65, 71, 10.86, 13.74, 16.2, 33, 17.21, 52, 66, 18.5, Kumāra 14.23, 33, 41, 43, 46, 49, 16.28, 29, 36, 17.29

Gañgā (गंगा)

Meaning/ Scientific term: The Ganges

Description: It is one of the major river of the Indian plain or northern India into Bangladesh, rises in the Western Himalayas in the Utarakhand state of India, and drains into the Sunderbans delta in the Bay of Bengal. It has long been considered as a holy river by Hindus and worship as the goddess Ganga in Hinduism. It has also been important historically, many provincial or imperial capitals (such as Pataliputra, Kanuj, Allahabad, Murshidabad and Calcutta) have been located on it banks.

Reference: Vik - 1, 1.10, 2.14, 3, 5.2, Abhi - 6, Megha - 63, Kumāra - 1.30, 54, 6.38, 57, 70, 7.41, 42, Raghu - 2.26, 4.32, 36, 73, 6.48, 10.37, 13.57, 14.3, 52, 16.33, 17.14

Gavākṣha (गवाक्ष)

Meaning/ Scientific term: Window

Description: A window is a shape in the wall of a building or in the side of a vehicle, which has glass in it so that light can come in and you can see out.

Reference: Raghu - 19.7

Graha/Grahamandala (ग्रह / ग्रहमन्डल)

Meaning/ Scientific term: Planet

Description: The term planet is ancient ties to history, science, mythology and religion. The planets were originally seen by many early cultures as divine or as emissaries of the gods. A planet basically is a celestial body orbiting a star (like sun) or stellar that is massire enough to be rounded by its own gravity, is not massive enough to cause there and nuclear fusion, and has cleared its neighbouring region of planets.

Reference: Mālā - 4, Śṛngāratilakam - 2

Granthi (ग्रन्थि)

Meaning/ Scientific term: Knot

Description: A knot is a method for fastening or securing linear material such as rope by tieing or interweaving. It may consist of a length of one or more segments of rope, string, and webbing, twine strap or even chain enter oven such that the line can bind to itself or to someother object, the 'Load'.

Different types of knots: tight interlacing of two ropes. A knot is also a unit of speed in aviation and marine navigation equal to one nautical mile per hour.

Halyard knot: interlacing of ropes used to attach the halyard to a sail.

Reef knot: interlacing of ropes made of two half-knots inverse to each other.

Bowline: interlacing of ropes with a loop that can be used as support.

Two round turns and a half: interlacing of ropes around an object by making two turns, then a half-knot.

Two half hitches: interlacing of ropes around an object by making two half-knots, one after the other.

Double shell bend: double interlacing of ropes, used to attach two ropes together.

Sheet knot: interlacing of ropes used to attach two ropes together.

Figure of eight knot: interlacing of ropes used to finish the end of a rope.

Overhand knot: simple interlacing of a rope.

Reference: Abhi - 6

Gṛhadirghikā (गृहदीर्घिका)

Meaning/ Scientific term: House-Pond

Description: It is a man-made small body of standing or stagnant water that is usually smaller than lake. A wide variety of man-made house pond i.e., bodies of water are classified as pond, including water gardens designed for aesthetic ornamentation, fish ponds designing for commercial fish breeding and cultivation, and solar ponds designed to store thermal energy.

According to limologist and fresh water biologists have proposed formal or definitions for pond, in part to include 'bodies of water where light (solar energy, natural sunlight) penetrates to the bottom of the waterbody'.

Reference: Raghu - 9.37

Guḍ (गुड़)

Meaning/ Scientific term: Molasess (mellāceum, from mel, mellishoncy)

Description: Molasass is a viscous by product of the processing of sugar cane or sugar beets into sugar. The 'molasses' comes from mel, the latin word for 'honey'. The quality of molasses depends on the maturity of the sugar cane or sugar beet extract (i.e., the amount of sugar sap extracted) and the method of extraction.

Reference: Ṛtu - 5.16

H

Haṃsa/Haṃsi/Rājhaṃsa (हंस / हंसी)

Meaning/ Scientific term: Swan

Description: Swans, genus Cygnus are birds of the family Anatidae which also includes geese and ducks. The swans are the largest members of the duck family Anatidae and are amongst the largest flying birds.

Reference: Raghu - 4.19, 5.75, 6.26, 8.59, 14.28, 16.54, 56, 17.25, 19.40, Vik - 1.20, 4, 4.14, Ṛtu - 1.5, 3.1, 2, 8, 11, 13, 16, 17, 21, 24, 25, 4.4, Megha - 11, 23, Kumāra - 1.30, Nalo - 1.24, 1.26, Śruto - 6, 17

Haricandana (हरिचन्दन)

Meaning/ Scientific term: Sandal wood, Indian Sandalwood, (*Santalum album*)

Description: Sandalwood is the name of different fragrant wood. These woods are yielded by trees in the genus Santalum, which are often used for the essential oil of contains. The wood is heavy and yellow in colour as well as fine-graused, and unlike many other aromatic wood's retains its fragrance for decades. Sandalwood has been valued and treasured for many years for its fragrance, carving, medical and religious qualities.

Reference: Raghu - 6.60

Harit (हरित)

Meaning/ Scientific term: The Green colour

Description: The Green colour or green paint. Naturally the leaves of kundri are used to make the natural green paint. The leaves are collected and crushed by a pastle. The colour is sequeezed out and collected in a coconut sheel. The colour is dried in the sun and then natural glue is added to it. This natural green colour is largely used by the rural patachitra painters.

Reference: Raghu - 3.22, 3.30, Abhi - 6.2

Haritāla (हरिताल)

Meaning/ Scientific term: Orpiment

Description: Orpiment is one of the 320 arsenic bearing minerals in nature. It is a common monoclinic arsenic sulfide mineral. Orpiment is an orange to yellow mineral that is found worldwide, and occurs as a sublimation product in volcanic fumaroles, low temperature hydrothermal vent, hot springs and as a byproduct of the decay of another arsenic mineral, realgar. It is often found in association with realgar and its chemical formula is As_2S_3.

Hema (हेम)

Meaning/ Scientific term: Gold (*Au, atomic no 79*)

Description: Gold is a chemical element with the symbol Au (from Latin: aurum (gold) and an atomic number of 79. It has been a highly sought-after precious metal for coinage, jewelery, and other arts since the beginning of recorded history. The native metal occurs as nuggets or grains in rocks, in veins and in alluvial deposits. Less commonly, it occurs in minerals as gold compounds, usually with tellurium. Gold metal is dense, soft, shiny and the most malleable and ductile pure metal known. Pure gold has a bright yellow color and luster traditionally considered attractive, which it maintains without oxidizing in air or water. Gold is one of the coinage metals and has served as a symbol of wealth and a store of value throughout history. Gold standards have provided a basis for monetary policies. It also has been linked to a variety of symbolisms and ideologies.

Although primarily used as a store of value, gold has many modern industrial uses including dentistry and electronics. Gold has traditionally found use because of its good resistance to oxidative corrosion and excellent quality as a conductor of electricity.

Chemically, gold is a transition metal. Compared with other metals, pure gold is chemically least reactive, resisting individual acids but being attacked by the acid mixture aqua regia, so named because it dissolves gold. Gold also dissolves in alkaline solutions of cyanide, which have been used in mining. Gold dissolves in mercury, forming amalgam alloys. Gold is insoluble in nitric acid, which dissolves silver and base metals, a property that has long been used to confirm the presence of gold in items, and this is the origin of the colloquial term 'acid test', referring to a gold standard test for genuine value.

Reference: Raghu - 10.51, 61, 1.10, 2.36, Megha - 15, 62, Raghu - 12.71, 15.30, 16.7, 17.10, 46, 19.41, Mālā - 3.21, Vik - 2, 5.2, 19, Ṛtu - 6.7, 24, Puṣpavanavilāsa - 10.26

Himālaya (हिमालय)

Meaning/ Scientific term: Himālaya mountain

Description: A mountain is a large land form that stretches above the surroundings land in a limited area usually in the form of peak. A mountain is generally steeper than till. Or a natural elevation of the earth surface rising more or less abruptly from the surroundings level and waiting an attitude which, relatiaty to the adjacent elevation is impressive or notable.

Reference: Kumāra - 1.1, 6.29

Himāṁśu (हिमांशु)

Meaning/ Scientific term: Moon

Description: The Moon is the Earth's only natural satellite and the fifth largest satellite in the solar system. The average distance (centre to centre) from the Earth to the Moon is 384,403 km., which is about thirty times the diameter of the Earth. The Moon makes a complete orbit around the Earth every 27.3 days (the orbital period), and the periodic variations in the geometry of the Earth-Moon-Sun system are responsible for the phases of the Moon, which repeat every 29.5 days (the synodic period). The Pull of gravity at its surface is about 17 percent of that at the Earth's surface. The Moon is the only celestial body on which human beings have made a manned landing.

Reference: Raghu - 5.16, 6.47

Hiranya/Hiranmaya (हिरन्य / हिरन्मय)

Meaning/ Scientific term: Gold

Description: *See* Hema

Reference: Raghu - 5.29, 6.53, 15.61, 17.26, 18.25

I

Ikṣu (इक्षु)

Meaning/ Scientific term: Sugarcane (*Saccharum officinarum*)

Description: Sugarcane is a sail tropical plant. It is grown for the sugar that can be obtained from its thick stem.

Reference: Ṛtu - 5.16, Raghu - 4.20

Indibara (इन्दिवर)

Meaning/ Scientific term: Lotus

Description: *See* Abja

Reference: Raghu - 13.54, 6.65, Ṛtu - 2.12, Śṛngāratilakam - 6, 19

Indu/Induvimba (इन्दु)

Meaning/ Scientific term: Moon

Description: *See* Himāṁśu

Reference: Raghu - 6.2, 53, 8.1, 8.15, 13.38, 15.54, 16.65, 18.37, 19.51, Mālā - 4, Vik - 2.9, Abhi - 3.2, 3, 4.5, Ṛtu - 5.3, Śruto - 35, Śṛngāratilakam - 9

Ingudi (इंगुदि)

Meaning/ Scientific term: Fruit (*Terminalia catappa*) Indian almond

Description: Tropical Almond. The seed is perhaps one of the more commonly found sea-beans washed ashore in *Tarminalia catappa* is a large tropical tree in the leadwood tree family, combretaceae. The tree has been spread widely by humans.

Common names include, Bengal almond, Malaber almond, Indian almond, Tropical almond, Sea almond etc. The *Terminalia catappa* has corky, light fruit that is disperced by water. The nut within the fruit is edible when fully ripe, tasting almost like almond. *Terminalia catappa* is widely grown in tropical regions of the world as an ornamental tree grown for the deep shade its large leaves provide. The fruit is edible, tasting slightly, acidic. The leaves contain several flavonoids, several tranins (such as punicalin, punicalagin) or Saponinc and phytosteriods. Due to this chemical agents, the leaves (also the bark) are used in different traditional medicines for various purposes. For instances, in Taiwan fallen leaves are used to treat lever diseases.

Reference: Abhi - 2, 4

J

Jāla/Jālaka (जाल / जालक)

Meaning/ Scientific term: Net

Description: It is a material made of twine or cord woven or tied together, with spaces in between usually used for catching fish or bird or insects.

Reference: Raghu - 7.9, 16.20, 19.40, Vik - 3.2, Abhi - 1.28, 7.16, Ṛtu - 1.19, 6.27, Śrngāratilakam - 8

Jalada/Jaladhi/Jala (जलद / जलधि / जल)

Meaning/ Scientific term: Cloud

Description: *See* Ambhasa

Reference: Kumāra - 1.14, Vik - 4, Raghu - 11.11, Abhi - 7.33, Megha (Purva) - 13, Ṛtu - 3.12, 6.3, Nalo - 3, Śṛngāratilakam - 13

Jalanidhi (जलनिधि)

Meaning/ Scientific term: Cloud

Description: *See* Jalada

Reference: Raghu - 6.85

Jambū (जम्बु)

Meaning/ Scientific term: Black plum - *Syzygium cumine*, Rose apple tree, (*Engenia Jambolana*)

Description: Rose apple tree is a member of the myrtle family, Myrtaceae, and is technically known as *Syzygium jambos* Alston. The term "rose apple" is so widely employed that the species has alternate names apart from those in the many local dialects of Africa, india. Malaya, southeastern Asia, the East Indies and Oceania. It is sometimes called 'Jaman' in India. The rose apple tree is native to the East Indies and Malaya and is cultivated and naturalized in many parts of India, Ceylon and former Indo-China and the Pacific Islands. It was introduced into Jamica in 1762 and become in Bermuda, the Bahamas and the West Indies and at low and medium elevations, from southern Mexico to Peru. In India, thc yield of mature rose apple tree will be a lot of fruit each season. The fruits are very light in weight because they are hollow, but this is a very small return for a tree that occupies so many places.

Reference: Megha - 21, 25

Jantu (जन्तु)

Meaning/ Scientific term: Animal

Description: Animals are a major group of multicellular, eukaryotic organisms of the kingdom Animalia or Metazoa. All animals are also heterotrops, meaning, they must ingest other organisms for sustenance. All animals have eukaryotic cells, sourrounded by a characteristic extracellular matrix composed of collagen and elastic glycoproteins.

Reference: Abhi - 5.2

Joytsnā (जोतस्ना)

Meaning/ Scientific term: The Moonlight

Description: The light of the moon i.e., the light which comes from the earth's only natural satellite moon, usually at night.

Reference: Raghu - 10.37, Abhi - 3, 4, Ṛtu - 3.7

Jvara (ज्वर)

Meaning/ Scientific term: Body temperature due to fever

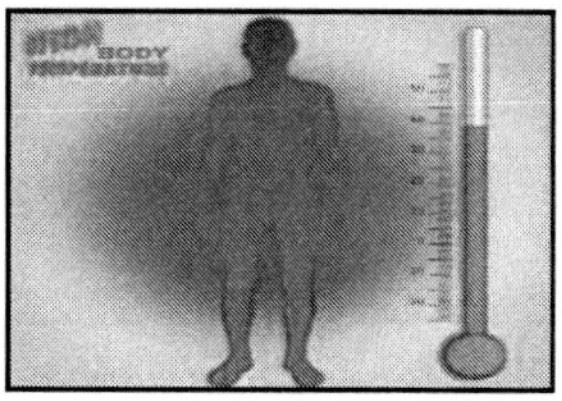

Description: It is a common medical sign characterized by an elevation of Temparature above the normal range of 98-100 °F due to increase in the body temperature regulatory 'set point'. A fever is one of the body's iminune responses which attempts to nentratire a bacterial or viral infection. People develop higher temperature with activities but this is not considered a fever as the set-point is normal.

Reference: Raghu - 8.84

Jyā (ज्या)

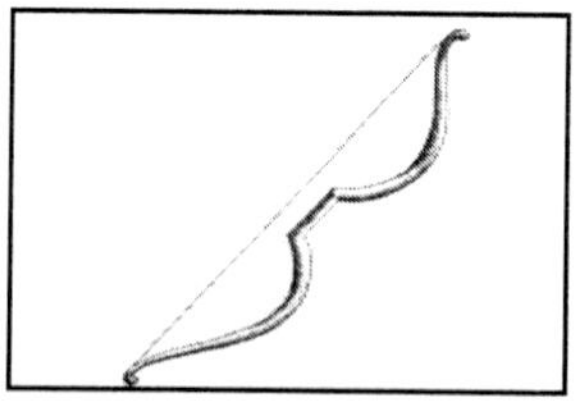

Meaning/ Scientific term: Bow

Description: Primitive weapen for hunting

Reference: Raghu - 9.64, 11, 77, 40, 16.84, Abhi - 2.4, 6, 3.1, Ṛtu - 6.38

Jyoti/Jyotiṣka/Jyotirlekhā/Kiraṇ (ज्योति / जोतिष्क / जोर्तिलेख / किरण)

Meaning/ Scientific term: Ray

Reference: Raghu - 2.75, 6.22, 7.36, 10.2, 23, 66, 11.21, 13.4, 68, 15.52, 59, 82, 17.35, Abhi - 1.23, 5.30, Raghu - 16.83, 17.35, Śṛngāratilakam - 26

K

Kadali/Kandali (कदलि / कन्दलि)

Meaning/ Scientific term: Banana/Plaintain Tree

Description: Banana is the common name for herbaceous plants of the genus *Musa* and for the fruit they produce. Banana comes in a variety of sizes and colours when ripe including colour yellow, purple and red.

Bananas are native to tropical Southeast Asia, and are likely to have first domesticated in Papua New Guinea. Today they are cultivated throughout the tropics. They are grown in a lot of countries round the Globe.

Reference: Kumāra - 1.36, Raghu - 12.96, Megha - 22, Ṛtu - 2.5

Kadamba (कदम्ब)

Meaning/ Scientific term: Fruit (*Neolamarckia cadamba*)

Description: Kadamba trees and flowers are also a universal favourite among the Gods. Krishna loved to sport in Kadamba forests, and the Mother Goddess Durga resides in a Kadamba forest (*Kadamba vana vasini*).

Reference: Abhi - 2.6, 6, Ṛtu - 2.17, 21, 24, 3.13, 4.9, Kumāra - 3.68, Megha - 27, Raghu - 13.27, 15.99

Kalamā (कलमा)

Meaning/ Scientific term: A type of Paddy, Asian rice, *Oryza sativa*

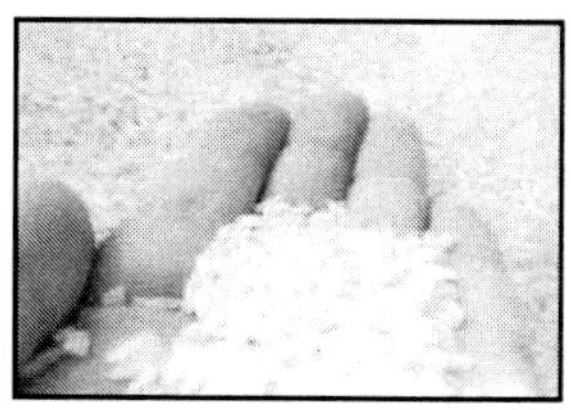

Description: The Paryayaratnamala, the Āryasaptasati, the Abhidhanaratnamala and the Krsiparasara tells us about paddy cultivation in Bengal. According to one scholar, 11 varieties of rice grew in the 24-Parganas. Ibn Batuta states that Bengal is a vast country and abounds in rice. Some terracotta plaques found at Paharpur depict paddy fields. It is interesting to note that varieties of rice are grown in Bengal. The Amarkosa refers to three varieties of paddy, Kalama Sastika, asuveribi (also called patala). Varahamihira adds four kinds of paddy viz. Kalama, red rice, yellow rice and hog's rice.

Reference: Raghu - 4.37

Kamala (कमल)

Meaning/ Scientific term: Lotus; Red lotus *Nelumbo nucifera*

Description: The (red) lotus has pride of place in Indian literature. The national flower is another universal favourite of the Gods. and its beauty is often used in similes for the beauty of heros/heroine's face as beautiful as a 'blooming lotus' or 'eyes shaped like lotus petals'. A woman's beauty may be compared to that of a pond full of blooming lotuses *Nalinī, padminī* or her slender frame to that of a lotus stem. A famous couplet ascribed to Kālidāsa describes a woman's face as a miracle of flower blooming within a flower: her beautiful eyes are like dark blue lotuses blooming in the pink lotus of her face! The goddess Lakshmi sits on a red Lotus, and Sarasvati, on a white one. The Lotus is associated with Lord Brahmā, who was created sitting on a lotus arising from the navel of Lord Vishnu. The lotus has esoteric and sacred significance in spirituality. The Mother Goddess (Devi) is called *Kamalāmba* or Lotus Mother: she resides in a thousand-petalled lotus said to be located in the *Sahasra Chakra* in the head. Raising the serpent power *kundalini* to this place leads to Realization, which is the aim of the practitioner of 'Sri Vidya Upasana'. Lotus symbols are central in Yantra patterns. and form part of many designs of decoration in more secular contexts. The lotus blooms at day and closes it night: so the sun is referred to as the 'Friend of the Lotus'.

Reference: Vik - 2.1, Abhi - 5.1, Ṛtu -1.28, 3.23, 5.13, 6.32, Nalo - 2.4, Śṛngāratilakam - 1, 8

Kampam (कम्पम्)

Meaning/ Scientific term: Vibration

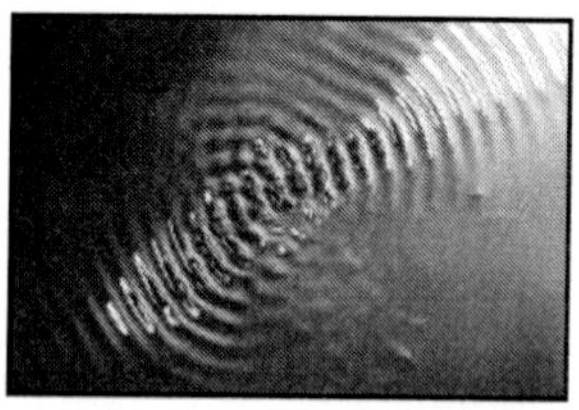

Description: Vibration refers to mechanical oscillations about an equilibrium point. The oscillations may be periodic such as the motion of a pendulum or random such as the movement of a tire on a gravel road.

Vibration is occasionally "desirable". For example the motion of a tuning fork, the reed in a woodwind instrument or harmonica, or the cone of a loudspeaker is desirable vibration, necessary for the correct functioning of the various devices. The study of sound and vibration are closely related. Sound or "pressure waves", are generated by vibrating structures (e.g. vocal cords); these pressure waves can also induce the vibration of structures (e.g. ear drum). Hence, when trying to reduce noise it is often a problem in trying to reduce vibration.

Reference: Raghu - 15.24

Kanaka/Rajat (कनक / रजत)

Meaning/ Scientific term: Gold

Description: *See* Kāncana

Reference: Raghu - 7.28, 19.56, Abhi - 3.11, Ṛtu - 1.26, 3.4, 5.13

Kānan/Vitān (कानन / वितान)

Meaning/ Scientific term: Garden

Description: A garden is a planned space, usually outdoors, set aside for the display, cultivation and enjoyment of plants and other forms of nature. The garden can incorporates both natural and man-made materials. The most common form is known as a residential garden.

Reference: Raghu - 12.27, 18.37, Vik - 4.35, Nalo - 2.50

Kāncana (कान्चन)

Meaning/ Scientific term: Gold

Description: *See* Hema

Reference: Kumāra - 8.29, Raghu - 6.79, 8.21, 13.33, 14.7, 16.70, Mālā - 2.9, Abhi - 6.6, 7.12, Ṛtu - 3.19, 4.4

Kandara (कन्दर)

Meaning/ Scientific term: Water logged land

Description: An area of low lying land which remains waterlogged. Waterlogging refers to the saturation of soil with water. Soil may be regarded as waterlogged when the water table of the groundwater is too high to conveniently permit an anticipated activity, like agriculture.

Reference: Vik - 1.17, 4

Kapi (कपि)

Meaning/ Scientific term: Monkey (*Macaca mulatta*)

Description: The Crab-eating macaque (Macacafascicularis) is a primarily arboreal macaque native to Southeast Asia. It is also called the cynomolgus monkey, Philippine monkey and the long-tailed macaque. The scientific name of the crab-eating macaque is Macaco fascicularis. This animal has several common names. It is often referred to as the long-tailed macaque because its tail is usually about the same length as its body and because its long tail distinguishes it from most other macaques. The species is also commonly known as the crab-eating macaque. Another common name for Macaca fascicularis is the cynomolgus monkey, which literally means 'dog-milker' monkey; this is the name most commonly used in laboratory settings. In Indonesia, Macaca fascicularis and other macaque species are known generically as kera, possibly because of the high-pitched alarm calls they give when in danger.

Reference: Ṛtu - 1.23, Raghu - 12.62, 14.19, 15.58

Kardama (कर्दम)

Meaning/ Scientific term: Mud

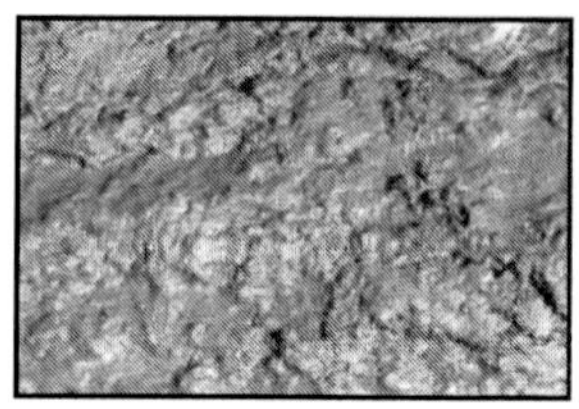

Description: Mud is a liquid or semi-liquid mixture of water and some combination of soil, silt, and clay. Ancient mud deposits harden over geological time to form sedimentary rock such as shale or mudstone (generally called lutites). Mud is closely related to slurry and sediment. Mud is similar to muck, but lacking significant quantities of humus, and often containing higher proportions of sand.

Reference: Ṛtu - 1.19

Karnikāra (कर्निकार)

Meaning/ Scientific term: A kind of flower *Cassia fistula*

Description: Hindi: Amaltas English: Golden Shower, Indian laburnum. Native to Southern Asia, from Southern Pakistan East through India to Myanrnar and South to Sri Lanka.

Reference: Vik - 2.22, 3.3, Kumāra - 3.28, 53, 62, Ṛtu - 6.6, 22, 29

Karoujasa (करौजस)

Meaning/ Scientific term: Strength

Description: Physical strength is the ability of a person or animal to exert force on physical objects using muscles. Increasing physical strength is the goal of strength training. An individual's physical strength is determined by two factors; the cross-sectional area of musclefibres recruited to generate force and the intensity of the recruitment. Individuals with a high proportion of type I slow twitch muscle fibers will be relatively weaker than a similar individual with a high proportion of type II fast twitch fibers, but would have a greater inherent capacity for physical endurance. The genetic inheritance of muscle fiber type sets the outermost boundaries of physical strength possible (barring the use of enhancing agents such as testosterone), though the unique position within this envelope is determined by training. Individual muscle fiber ratios can be determined through a muscle biopsy. Other considerations are the ability to recruit muscle fibers for a particular activity, joint angles, and the length of each limb. For a given cross-section, shorter limbs are able to lift more weight. The ability to gain muscle also varies person to person, based mainly upon genes dictating the amounts of hormones secreted, but also on sex, age, health of the person, and adequate nutrients in the diet.

Reference: Raghu - 9.2

Kārpāsak (कार्पासक)

Meaning/ Scientific term: Cotton plant - *Gossypium.* See also Aṁsuk

Description: Cotton is a natural fiber harvested from the cotton plant. Cotton is one of the oldest fibers under human cultivations with traces of witon over 7000 years old recovered from archaeological sites. Cotton is in the "mallon" family and produces delicate, lovely flowers.

Cotton is a soft, staple fiber that grows in a form known as a boll around the seeds of the cotton plant, a shrub native to tropical and subtropical regions around the world, including the Americas, India and Africa. The fiber most often in spurn into yarn or thread and used to make a soft textile, breathable textile, which is the most widely used natural - fiber cloth in clothing today.

Reference: Raghu - 9.43, Vik - 5.12, Ṛtu - 4.3, 4, 17, 6.4, 21

Kāśa (काश)

Meaning/ Scientific term: Species of grass

Description: Kans grass (*Saccharum spontaneum*) is a grass native to South Asia. It is a perennial grass, growing up to three meters in height, with spreading rhizomatous roots.

In the Terai-Duar grasslands, a lowland ecoregion at the base of the Himalaya range in Nepal, India and Bhutan, kans grass quickly colonises exposed silt plains created each year by the retreating monsoon floods, forming almost pure stands on the lowest portions of the floodplain. Kans grasslands are an important habitat for the Indian rhinoceros (*Rhinoceros unicornis*). In Nepal, kans grass is harvested to thatch roofs or fence vegetable gardens.

Elsewhere, its ability to quickly colonize disturbed soil to become an invasive species that takes over croplands and pasturelands. *Saccharum spontaneum* has a considerable number of regional names in South Asia, for instance kash being common in Bengali.

Reference: Kumāra - 7.11, Raghu - 4.17, Ṛtu - 3.1, 2, 28

Kāṭha (काठ)

Meaning/ Scientific term: Wood

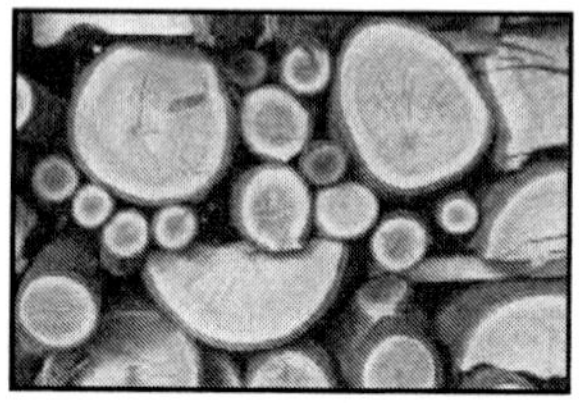

Description: Wood is a hard, fibrous tissue found in many plants. It has been used for centuries for both fuel and as a construction material for several types of living areas such as horses, known as carpentry. Wood is yielded by trees, which increase in diameters by the formation, between the existing wood and the inner bark, of new woody layers which envelop the entire stem, living branches, and roots. Technically this is known as secondary growth, it is the result of cell division in the vascular cambium, a lateral meristem and subsequent expansion of the new cells. Wood is an organic material, a natural composite of cellulose fibers (which are strong in tension) embedded in a matrix of lignin which resists compression. In the strict sense wood is produced as secondary, xylem in the stems of trees (and other woody plant). Wood may also refer to other plant materials with comparable properties, and to materials engineered from wood or wood chips or fiber. People have used wood for millennia for many purposes, primarily as a fuel or as a construction material for making houses, tools, weapons, furniture, packaging, artworks and paper.

Reference: Mālā - 4, Abhi - 6

Kaustuva (कौस्तुभ)

Meaning/ Scientific term: Jewel

Description: A Jewel is a precious stone used to decorate valuable things that we wear, such as rings or neckless etc.

Reference: Raghu - 10.10, 10.62, 17.29

Ketaka/Ketakī (केतक / केतकि)

Meaning/ Scientific term: The flower Kewdā (*Pandanus odoratissimus*)

Description: A fragrant flower used in making perfume and aromatic oil, Ketaki is not used in worship: it is supposedly cursed by Lord Shiva for bearing false witness of Lord Brahma.

Reference: Kumāra - 8.58, Megha - 23

Khani (खनि)

Meaning/ Scientific term: Mine

Description: It is a place where minerals may be olotamed, abundantly either by excavation or by washing the soil. The excavation made in the earth for the purpose of extracting ores, coal, precious stones etc.

Reference: Raghu - 17.66, 18.22

Kharjura (खर्जुर)

Meaning/ Scientific term: A kind of Date Palm

Description: *Phoenix sylvestris (sylvestris* - Latin, of the forest) also known as Silver Date Palm or Sugar Date Palm, is a species of flowering plant in the palm family native to southern Pakistan, most of India and Bangladesh. Growing in plains and scrubland to 1300 m, the fruit from this palm species is used to make wine and jelly. The sap is tapped and drunk fresh or fermented into toddy. The fresh sap is boiled to make palm jaggery in West Bengal state of India and Bangladesh. *Phoenix sylvestris* ranges from 4 to 15 m in height and 40 cm in diameter; not as large as the Canary Island Date Palm, but nearly so. and resembling it. The leaves are 3 m long gently recurved, on I m petioles with acanthophylls near the base. The leaf crown grows to 10 m wide and 7.5 to 10 m tall containing up to 100 leaves. The single-seeded fruit ripens to a purple-red colour.

Reference: Raghu - 4.57

Kicaka (किचक)

Meaning/ Scientific term: Hollow bamboo, Indian bamboo *Bambusa vulgaris*

Description: Bamboo is a group of perennial evergreens in the true grass family Poaceae, subfamily Bambusoideae, tribe Bambuseae. Giant bamboos are the largest members of the grass family. In bamboo, the internodal regions of the stem are hollow and the vascular bundles in the cross section are scattered throughout the stem instead of in a cylindrical arrangement.

Bamboo is one of the fastest-growing plants on Earth. It has been measured surging skyward as fast as 100 cm in a 24-hour period due to a unique rhizome-dependent system. However, the growth rate is dependent on local soil and climatic conditions. Primarily growing in regions of warmer climates during the Cretaceous period, vast fields existed in Asia. Bamboo is also known to be able to grown over 100 feet tall. Bamboos are of notable economic and cultural significance in South Asia, South East Asia and East Asia, being used for building materials, as a food source and as a versatile raw product.

Reference: Megha - 60, Raghu - 2.12, 4.73

Kiṁsuk/Kiṁshuka/Kinshuka (किंशुक)

Meaning/ Scientific term: Palas flower/Botanical name: *Butea monosperma* Family: Fabaceae (pea family) Synonyms: *Butea frondosa, Erythrina monosperma, Plaso monosperma*

Description: Flower Palash is 'Kiṁgshuk' in Sanskrit and 'Flame of Forest' or 'Parrot Tree' in English. Rabindranath had used the term 'Kingshuk' in his songs to immortalize spring. The term 'Flame of Forest' is also cognizable, as large tracts of forest of Palash can be found in Jharkhand and Chattisgarh, which literally flames up when Palash bloom. The term 'Parrot Tree' is pretty interesting; we shall come to that later in this article. Palash after all is the ultimate statement of spring in this part of the world. It is very much a native tree of Birbhum also Purulia. Very near Santiniketan, the Goalpara village is home to fairly large numbers of Palash. But the only easily visible Yellow Palash can be found beside Hatipukur at Santiniketan. These flowers, which are scentless, are massed along the ends of the stalks-dark velvety green like the cup-shaped calices- and the brilliance of the stiff, bright flowers is shown off to perfection by this deep, contrasting colour. Each flower consists of five petals comprising with one standard, two smaller "wings" and a very curved beak-shaped keel. It is this keel which gives it the name of Parrot Tree. In olden days, the flowers of Tesu were used to make color for the festival of Holi.

Reference: Ṛtu - 6.21, 22, Raghu - 9.31

Kokila (कोकिल)

Meaning/ Scientific term: Cuckoo/Asian Koel *Eudynamys scolopaceus*

Description: A Cuckoo is a bird that has a call of two quick notes, and lays its egg in other birds nest.

Reference: Mālā - 3.4, Ṛtu - 6.22, 26, 29, 35, 37, Abhi - 6.4, Śṛngāratilakam - 2, Kumāra- 3.32, 4.14, 16, Puṣpavānavilāsa - 8, 26

Kraunca (क्रोन्च)

Meaning/ Scientific term: Bird/Pond Heron or Paddybird (*Ardeola grayii*)

Description: The Indian Pond Heron or Paddybird (*Ardeola grayii*) is a small heron. It is of old origins, breeding in southern Iran and east to India, Burma, Bangladesh and Sri Lanka. They are widespread and common but can be easily missed when the stalk prey at the edge of small water-bodies or even when the root closed to human habitations. They are however distinctive when put to flight, the bright white wings flashing in contrast to the cryptic streaked olive and brown colours of the body. They are very common in India, and are usually solitary but numbers of them may sometimes feed in close proximity during the dry seasons when small wetlands have a high concentration of prey. They are semi-colonial breeders. They may also forage at garbage heaps. During dry seasons, they sometimes take to foraging on well watered lawns or even dry grassland.

The Indian Pond Heron's feeding habitat is marshy wetlands. They usually feed at the edge of ponds but make extensive use of floating vegetation such as Water hyacinth to access deeper water. They may also on occasion swim on water or catch fish from the air and land in deeper waters. They have also been observed to fly and capture fishes leaping out of water. Sometimes, they fly low over water to drive frogs and fishes towards the shore before settling along the shoreline. The primary food of these birds includes crustaceans, aquatic insects, fishes, tadpoles and sometimes leeches. Outside wetlands, these herons feed on insects (including crickets, dragonfly and bees), fish (Barilius noted as important in a study in Chandigarh) and amphibians.

Reference: Ṛtu - 4.8, 19, 5.1

Kṛsi Phalam (कृषिफलम)

Meaning/ Scientific term: Agricultural produce of a crop

Description: Agricultural produce is the annual or season's, yield of any plant that is grown in-significant qualities to be harvested as food as Livestock fodder, fuel, or for any other economic purpose. There are many types of crops that are used for industrial purposes. Crops are grown and harvested for the sole purpose of making profit and food for people, as they are grown in large amounts (in case of any staple food) in a certain area suitable for growing crops.

Reference: Megha (Purva) - 16

Kṛṣṇasāra (कृष्णसार)

Meaning/ Scientific term: Black Deer

Description: Blackbuck (*Antilope cervicapra*), is a species of antelope native to the Indian subcontinent. This species is the only member of the genus Antilope. It is one of the fastest of all terrestrial animals reaching to speeds of up to 80 km/h and is one of the few antelopes where males and females have distinctive coloration, as the male bucks are a distinctive black and white and have long twisted horns, while females are fawn coloured with no horns. The blackbuck is the provincial animal of India it is known as Krishna Mriga in Kannada. Also known as Krishna Jinka in Telugu, it has been declared as the state animal of Andhra Pradesh. Other local names for the species include Krishnasar in Bengali, Kala Hiran, Sasin, Iralai Maun, and Kalveet in Marathi. The distinctive horns of the Blackbuck are ringed with 1 to 4 spiral turns, rarely more than 4 turns, and can be as long as 79cm (31 in). A trophy Blackbuck is greater than 46cm (18 in). In the male, the upper body is black (dark brown), and the belly and eye rings are white. The light-brown female is usually hornless. Blackbuck usually roams the plains in herds of 15 to 20 animals with one dominant male.

The diet of the Blackbuck consists mostly of grasses, although it does eat pods, flowers and fruits to supplement its diet. The maximum life span recorded is to years and the average is 12 years. Today the blackbuck population is confined to areas in Maharashtra, Orissa, Punjab, Rajasthan, Haryana, Gujarat, Andhra Pradesh, Tamil Nadu and Karnataka with a few small pockets in Central India. Their range decreased sharply during the 20th century. Since 2003, the International Union for Conservation of Nature (IUCN) lists the species as near threatened.

Reference: Kumāra - 3.36, Vik - 4.57, Abhi - 1, Raghu - 9.55, 13.34, Śṛngāratilakam-18

Kṛttikā (कृत्रिका)

Meaning/ Scientific term: Nakṣatra

Description: The star cluster Krttikā, popularly transliterated (Krittika) sometimes known as Kartika, corresponds to the open star cluster Pleiades in Indian astronomy and Jyotiṣa in Indian astrology. The name literally translates to "the cutters".

In mythology:

According to Hindu mythology, the god Murugan was raised by the six sisters known as the Krttikā and thus came to be known as Kārtikeya (literary "Him of the Kartika"). According to the Mahabharata, Murugan was born to Agni and Svaha, after the latter impersonated six of the seven wives of the Saptarshi and made love to him. The Saptarshi, hearing of this incident and doubting their wives' chastity, divorced them. These wives then became the Krttikā.

Reference: Raghu - 14.22

Kṣara/Kṣāra (क्षर / क्षार)

Description: Soil with a 'ot value' higher than 73 is normally refers to as alkaline in nature. This soil property can occur naturally, due to the presence of alkali salts. Although some plants do prefer slightly basic soil, most and alkaline-soils can cause problems.

Reference: Raghu - 8.9

Kuliśa (कुलिश)

Meaning/ Scientific term: Thunderbolt

Description: A thunderbolt is another term for a discharge of lightning or a symbolic representation thereof. As divine manifestation it has been a powerful symbol throughout history and has appeared in many mythologies lightning plays a role in many mythologies, often as the weapon of a sky and storm god. In Hindu mythology, the god Indra is known as the god of lightning. His main weapon is the thunderbolt (i.e., Vajra). In Greek mythology, the thunderbolt is a weapon given to Zeus by the Cyclops.

Reference: Raghu - 9.12

Kumkum (कुमकुम)

Meaning/ Scientific term: Saffron Paint/Origion Saffron

Description: It is a red pigment used by Hindu married woman to make a mark of marriage on the forehead.

The seeds of saffron are used to extract colour. The seeds grow in spiky pods which grow in clusters at the top of the tree. To make the Kumkum i.e. red-colour, the seed are removed from dried fruit pods, then the seeds are rubbed by hand and the colour is collected in a dried coconut shell. The coloured whitein is the dried in the sun and then natural glue is added to it, then Kumkum is ready to use for painting etc.

Reference: Vik - 4, Ṛtu - 5.9, 6.5, 14

Kumuda (कुमुद)

Meaning/ Scientific term: Lotus

Description: See Kamala

Reference: Raghu - 16.86, 81, 85, 17.1, 6.86, 18.3, 19.34, Ṛtu - 3.2, 15.21, 25, 28, Kumāra - 7.74, 8.70, Vik - 3.16, Abhi - 5.28

Kunda (कुन्द)

Meaning/ Scientific term: A kind of jasmine, Star jasmine (*Jasminum multiflorum/ pubescens*)

Description: In Indian mythology, Kund is known for its whiteness. So, instead of the common western phrase 'white as snow', what often appears in Hindu mythological stories is 'white as kunda'. Also, beautiful white teeth are often compared to Kunda buds. It is held to be especially sacred to Vishnu. In Manipur, Kunda flowers are used in worship, and are an essential part of a marriage ceremony. The bride garlands the groom with two flower garlands. The groom then takes one of the two and garlands the bride.

Reference: Megha - 51, 56, Vik - 2.4, Abhi - 5.19, Mālā - 3.8, Ṛtu - 4.2, 6, 31, Kumāra-17.27

Kuṇḍala (कुन्डल)

Meaning/ Scientific term: Ear ring

Description: Ear ring are jewelry attached to be the earlote or some other external part of the ear. Ear ring are used by men and women by both the sexes. Ear piercing is one of the oldest known forms of body modification, with artistic form. The written references are found from cultures around the world dating back to early history. One of the early sign of ear ring worn by men, one from persepolis in ancient Persia. The carved images of the soldiers from various parts of the Persian Empire which are displayed on some of the surviving walls of the palace showing the soldiers wearing an ear ring.

Reference: Ṛtu - 3.19

Kurabaka (कुरबक)

Meaning/ Scientific term: Blossom of red amaranth (*Barleria cristala*)

Description: *Barleria cristala* (Philippine violet, Bluebell barleria or Crested Philippine violet), is a plant of the Acanthaceae family.

Distribution and habitat:

It is native to a wide area ranging from Southern China to India and Myanmar. Cultivated as an ornamental plant in villages and gardens, it has become naturalized in Hawaii, where it grows in dry habitats. In Fiji, where it is known as 'tombithi' and in Christmas Island (Indian Ocean), the shrub grows also as a ruderal species along roadsides and disturbed areas from near sea level to about 100 m.

Description:

It grows as a shrub 60-100 cm tall. The leaves are dark green on the upper surface and pale green on the lower surface. They are elliptic to narrowly ovate. The flowers are about 5 cm long, funnel-shaped in violet, pink, or white color. The fruits are about 1.5 cm long'ellipsoid capsules. They become glabrous and glossy at maturity.

Reference: Megha - 18, Vik - 2.7, Raghu - 9.29, Mālā - 3.5, 9, Ṛtu - 6.20, 33

Kuśa (कुश)

Meaning/ Scientific term: Grass/*Pao cynosuroides*

Description: Grasses or 'graminoids', are monocotyledonous, usually herbaceous plants with narrow leaves growing from the base. The true grasses include cereals, bamboo and the grasses of lawns and *graeoland* (*srana*). They include the grasses of the Poaceae (or *Gramineae*) family, as well as the sedges (*Cyperaceae*) and the rules (*Jurcaceae*).

Reference: Raghu - 1.95, 9.21, 15.97, 16.1, 81, 88, 18.4, 19.2

Kuvalaya (कुवलय)

Meaning/ Scientific term: Waterlily/White Lotus

Description: A water lily is a plant with large flat leaves and colourful flowers which floats on the surface of lakes and rivers.

Reference: Megha - 48, Mālā - 4.10, Ṛtu - 2.23, Puṣ pavānavilāsa- 10

L

Lākshārasa (लाक्षरस)

Meaning/ Scientific term: (Lac) Shellac (*Laccifer Lacca*)

Description: Lac is the scarlet resineous secretion of a number of species of insects, namely some of the species of the genera Metatachardia, Laccifer, *Tachordiella*, Austrotacharidia, Afrotachardina, and Tachardina of the super family Coccoidea, of which the most commonly cultivated species is Kerria Lacca. The above-mentioned families are some of the 28 families of scale insects and mealybugs comprising a large group of about 8000 described species of plant sucking insects, a few of which produce similar natural products (e.g., cochineal and crimson). Thousands of these tiny insects colouire branches of suitable host trees and secrete the resinous pigment. The coated branches of the host trees are cut and harvested as sticklac.

The harvested sticklac is crushed and sieved to remove imparities. The sieved material is then repeatedly washed to remove insect parts and other soluble material. The resulting product is called Seedlac. The prefix seed refers to its pellet shape. Seedlac which still contains 3-5% impurities is processed into shellac by heat treatment or solvent extraction. It is used in vioiin and other varnish and is soluble in alcohol. The leading producer of lac is Jharkhand, followed by Chhattisgarh, West Bengal, and Maharastra. Lac production is also found in Bangladesh, Myanmer,Thailand, Laos, Vietnam and parts of China. It is also found in Mexico. The use of lac dye goes back to ancient time. It has been used in India as a skin cosmetic and dye- for wool and silk. In China it is a traditional dye for leather goods. The use of lac for dye has been supplanted by synthetic dyes. It is used in medicine as hepatoprotective and anliobesity drug.

Reference: Abhi - 4.5, Ṛtu - 6.15, Puṣpavānavilāsa - 22, Meghduta - 12

Latā/Latāvitapi Latāvitāna (लता / लताविटपि / लतावितान)

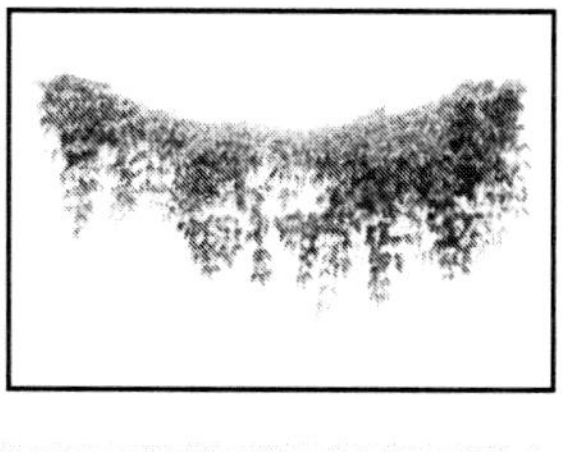

Meaning/Scientific term: Creeper (*Butea frondosa*)-*Butea monosperma*

Description: Creepers are plants with long stems that wind themselves around objects.

Reference: Vik - 1.18, 2.4, Abhi - 4.12, Ṛtu - 1.24

Lavana (लवन)

Meaning/ Scientific term: Salt/Nacl

Description: Salt is a strong-tasting substance, is the form of white powder or crystals, which is used to improve the flavour and taste of food or to preserve it. Salt occurs naturally in sea water.

Reference: Raghu - 12.70, 13.15, 15.2, 5, 17, 26, 38, 40, Vik - 1.19

Lavanga (लवंग)

Meaning/ Scientific term: Cloves, volatile oil

Description: Cloves (*Syzygium aromaticum; synonym Eugenia aromaticum or Eugenia caryophyllata*) are the aromatic dried flower buds of a tree in the family Myrtaceae. Cloves are native to Indonesia and used as a spice in cuisines all over the world. Cloves are now harvested primarily in Indonesia, Madagascar, Zanzibar, Pakistan, and Sri Lanka. They are also grown in India under the name Lavanga. The clove tree is an evergreen that grows to a height ranging from 8-12 m. having large square leaves and sanguine flowers in numerous groups of terminal clusters. The flower buds are at first of a pale color and gradually become green, after which they develop into a bright red, when they are ready for collecting. Cloves are harvested when 1.5-2 cm long and consist of a long calyx, terminating in four spreading sepals, and four unopened petals which form a small ball in the center.

Eugenol comprises 72-90% of the essential oil extracted from cloves, and is the compound most responsible for the cloves' aroma. Eugenol has pronounced antiseptic and anaesthetic properties. Of the dried buds, 15-20 percent is essential oils, and the majority of this is eugenol. A kilogram of dried buds yields approximately 150 ml of eugenol.

Cloves are used in Indian Ayurvedic medicine, Chinese medicine, and Western herbalism and dentistry, where the essential oil is used as an anodyne (painkiller) for dental emergencies. Cloves are used as a carminative, to increase hydrochloric acid in the stomach and to improve peristalsis. Cloves are also said to be a natural anthelmintic. The essential oil is used in aromatherapy when stimulation and warming are needed, especially for digestive problems. Topical application over the stomach or abdomen are said to warm the digestive tract. Clove oil, applied to a cavity in a decayed tooth, also relieves toothache. It also helps to decrease infection in the teeth due to its antiseptic properties.

Reference: Vik - 24, Abhi - 3, 6

Locana (लोचन)

Meaning/ Scientific term: Eye

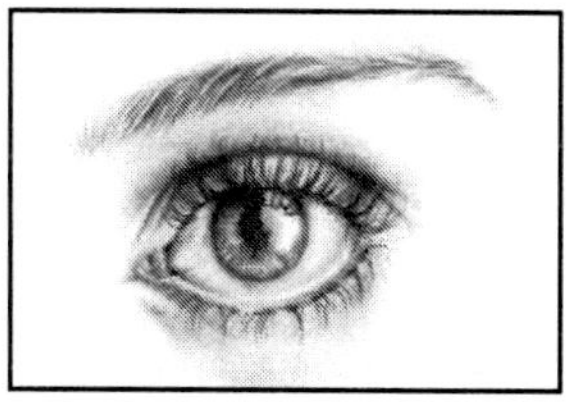

Description: It is the organ of animal body which detects light, and sends electrical impulses along the optic nerve to the visual and other areas of brain.

Eyes are organs that detect light, and convert it to electro-chemical impulses in neurons. The simplest photoreceptors in conscious vision connect light to movement. In higher organisms the eye is a complex optical system which collects light from the surrounding environment; regulates its intensity through a diaphragm; focuses it through an adjustable assembly of lenses to form an image; converts this image into a set of electrical signals; and transmits these signals to the brain, through corhplex neural pathways that connect the eye, via the optic nerve, to the visual cortex and other areas of the brain.

Reference: Raghu - 7.42, 11.93, 13.29, Mālā 4.8, Vik - 3.15, 4.8, Puṣpavānavilāsa - 12, Śṛngaratikakam - 24

Lodhra (लोध्र)

Description: Pale as Cosmetic Powder prepared from the bark of the tree Symplocos recemosa.

- *Botanical Name : Symplocos oacemosa*
- *Family Name :* Symplocaceae
- *Common Name :* Symplocos Bark
- *Part Used :* Bark
- *Habitat:* It is found in the plains and lower hills of North and East India and in Himalayas upto 1,400-m altitude
- *Product offered :* Bark

Uses : Bark is astringent, refrigerant, ophthalmic, expectorant, anti-inflammatory, hypothermic, astringent, depurative, febrifuge, haemostatic, stomachic and suppurative.

Bark is used to treat haemorrhage, acne and pimples, eye diseases, spongy and bleeding gums, leucorrhea, wounds, ulcers, tumors, leprosy, skin diseases, asthma, bronchitis, dropsy, arthritis, fever, menstrual disorders, liver diseases, menorrhagia, diarrhea, dysentery, and bowel complaints. A decoction of the bark or wood is used as a gargle for giving firmness to spongy and bleeding gums. It is one of the constituent of a plaster used to promote maturation of boils and other malignant growth.

This tree, in Sanskrit, was called Lodhra, Rodhra or Srimata meaning "propitious", and "Tilaka" because it was used in making the Tilaka mark on the forehead. A decoction of the bark was used for gargling when the gums were spongy and bleeding (Susruta). Roxburgh remarks that the bark was popular among the dyes of red in Calcutta and seemed to be used as a mordant only. In Europe it was formerly looked upon as a cinchona bark and had been known at various times as "Ecorce de lautour", "China nova", "China calafornica", "China Brasilarsis" and "China paraquatan". It was also known as "Lotus Bark".

Reference: Raghu 2.29, 3.2, Kumāra 7.9, 17

Lohita (लोहित)

Meaning/ Scientific term: Red Colour, Blood

Description: Blood is a specialized bodily fluid, composed of blood cells and blood plasma that delivers necessary substances to the body's cells - such as nutrients and oxygen and transports waste products away from those same cells. In terms of anatomy and histology, blood is considered a specialized form of connective tissue, given its origin in the bones and the presence of potential molecular fibers in the form of Fibrinogen. The blood cells present in the blood are mainly red blood cells (also called RBCs or erythrocyles) and white blood cells, including leutocyles and platelets. The most abundant cells in vertebrate blood are red blood cells. These contain hemoglobin, are iron-containing protein, which facilities transporation of oxygen by reversibly binding to this respiratory gas and greatly increasing its solubility in blood. Blood plasma, i.e. plasma, which constitutes 55% of blood fluid, is mostly water (90%) by volume, and contains dissolved proteins, glucose, minerals ions, Carbon-di-oxide, hormones, platelates and blood cells, themselves. Carbon-di-oxide is almost entirely transported extra cellulosely disolved in plasma as bi-carbonetion.

Reference: Vik - 5.4, Abhi - 1.28, Raghu - 4.81, 7.58, Abhi - 7.35, Kumāra - 8.75, 8.28, Abhi - 5.23, Ṛtu 1.21. In Kumārasambhava Lohitendu maṇi has only been mentioned as Candrakānta maṇi.

Louha (Luh) (लौह)

Meaning/ Scientific term: Iron/Fe

Description: This is a chemical element. Fe, atomic number 26, and atomic weight 55,847. Iron is the fourth most abundant element in the crist of the Earth. It is a malleable, tough, silvergray, magnetic metal. It melts 1540 c boils at 2800 c and has a density of 7.86 g/cm.

Reference: Kum - 2.59

M

Mādhavi (Mādhavi Latā) (माधवि / माधविलता)

Meaning/ Scientific term: Flower *Combretum indicum*

Description: In stories of Krishna, Madhavi-lata is found every where in Vrindavan. and creates a wonderful atmosphere with its fragrance and the three-colored flowers: This forest has Atimukta-trees therefore the chariot makers resort to it (chariots are made of the wood), the makers of Madhavi-garlands like it (*Atimukta* means Madhavi flower) and those who desire liberation come here (to Vrindavana; (*Atimukta* means completely liberated).

Reference: Puṣpavānavilāsa - 5

Madhu/Madhukar/Madhuka (मधु / मधुकर / मधुक)

Meaning/ Scientific term: Honey

Description: Honey is a sweet food made by bees using nectar from flowers. The variety produced by honey bees is the one most commonly referred to and is the type of honey collected by beekeepers and consumed by humans. Honey produced by other bees and insects has distinctly different properties.

Honey bees form nectar into honey by a process of regurgitation, and store it as a primary food source in wax honeycombs inside the beehive. Beekeeping practices encourage overproduction of honey so the excess can be taken from the colony.

Honey gets its sweetness from the monosaccharides fructose and glucose, and has approximately the same relative sweetness as that of granulated sugar. It has attractive chemical properties for baking, and a distinctive flavor that leads some people to prefer it over sugar and other sweeteners. Most microorganisms do not grow in honey because of its low water activity of 0.6. Honey has a long history of human consumption, and is used in various foods and beverages as a sweetener and flavoring. It also has a role in religion and symbolism. Flavors of honey vary based on the nectar source, and various types and grades of honey are available. It is also used in various medicinal traditions to treat ailments.

Reference: Raghu - 8.68, 9.7, 18.52, 19.46, Abhi - 2.11, 5.1, 6, Ṛtu - 1.3, 3.6, 6.20, 27, Kumāra - 7.14, Raghu - 6.25, Nalo - 2.2, 2.11, 2.15, 2.27, Vik - 4.42

Madhupa/Madhuliha (मधुप / मधुलिह)

Meaning/ Scientific term: Bee, *Apis cerana indica* Indian honey bee

Description: Bees are a monopoly letic lineage within the super family Apoidea, Presently Classified by the unranked on name Anthophila. They are the flying insects closely related to wasps and ants. Honey bees are highly social flying insects under genus *Apis* they are closely related to wasps and ants and are known for their role in pollination and for producing honey and bee wax.

Reference: Raghu - 15.15, Śṛngāraṣṭakam - 6

Maghava/Megha (मघव / मेघ)

Meaning/ Scientific term: Cloud

Description: A cloud is a visible mass or droplets or little drops of water or frozen crystals suspended in the atmosphere above the surface of the Earth or another planetary body. Clouds are studied in the nephrology or cloud physics branch of meteorology.

Reference: Vik - 5, Abhi - 7.26

Mahiṣa (महिष)

Meaning/ Scientific term: *Bubalus bubalis* (Ox) Baffalo (*Syncerus caffer*) African buffalo

Description: Asian buffalo, Bubalus, a genus that includes the domesticated water buffalo. The wild water buffalo, sometimes called the Arni, *Bubalus bulbalis*, is somewhat larger than the African buffalo. An adult male typically stands 1.5 to 1.9 meters (5 to 6.25 feet) tall at the shoulder and weighs 700 to 1200 kg, while females are smaller. The spread of their horns is the largest of any living ungulate. They are covered with sparse hair and range in color from light gray to black. Their skin is very thick, which helps to protect them from insects and from thorns. The wild water buffalo is native to the area of India and Southeast Asia, and domesticated.

Buffalos drink water every 24 hours and spend their time equally between resting and grazing. Vocal communication is important within buffalo society.

Reference: Raghu - 9.61, 16.13, Ṛtu - 1.21, Abhi - 2

Mahiṣodhi/Mahauṣodhi (महिषधि / महौषधि)

Meaning/ Scientific term: Herbal Medicine; medicinal plant

Description: Herbal medicine, sometimes referred to as botanical medicine or herbalism involves the use of plants, or parts of plants, to treat injuries or illnesses. This field also covers the use of herbs or botanicals to improve overall health and wellness. Herbalist, herbal medicine practitioners, traditional medicine practitioners, and Ayurvedic, homeopathic, and naturopathic healers all use herbal remedies in their practices.

Seeds, leaves, sterns, bark, roots, flowers, and extracts of all of these have been used in herbal medicine over the millennia of their use. These supplemental treatments have been delivered raw, in teas and tinctures, as topical applications, in liquid forms, and in pills and capsules. In the beginning the plants were consumed raw or combined with hot water as a soup or tea. Later, the plants were dried and crushed for other uses. The plants were found in the -wild and uses were often based on superstitious or visual cues. Plants were often used to treat body systems because they were shaped like that body part or because they grew in a particular area. As science began to take a closer look at herbal remedies, their use became more refined. Herbs, and other plants, are actually the precursors to many of today's medicinal drugs. Some of the pharmaceutical medications on the market are extracts of some of these traditional herbs.

Herbal medicines have been documented for almost 4000 years. These medicines have survived real world testing and thousands of years of human testing. Some medicines have been discontinued due to their toxicity, while others have been modified or combined with additional herbs to offset side effects. Many herbs have undergone changes in their uses. Studies conducted on the herbs and their effects keep changing their potential uses.

Reference: Kumāra - 1.2, 30

Makara (मकर)

Meaning/ Scientific term: A kind of animal/crocodile

Description: Makara (Sanskrit: मकर), is a sea-creature in Hindu mythology. It is generally depicted as half animal (in the frontal part in animal forms of elephant or crocodile or stag, or deer) and in hind part as aquatic creature, in the tail part, as a fish tail or also as seal. Sometimes, even a peacock tail is depicted.

Makara is the vāhana (vehicle) of the Ganga - the goddess of river Ganges (Ganga) and the sea god Varuna. It is also the insignia of the love-god Kāmadeva. Kamadeva's flag (dhvaja) is known as Karkadhvaja, a flag having makara depicted on it. Makara is the astrological sign of Capricorn, one of the twelve symbols of the Zodiac. It is often portrayed protecting entryways to Hindu and Buddhist temples.

Makara symbolized in ornaments are also in popular use as wedding gifts for bridal decoration. The Hindu Preserver-god Vishnu is also shown wearing makara-shaped earrings.

'Makara' is a Sanskrit word which means "sea dragon" or "water-monster" and in Tibetan language it is called the "chu-srin", and also denotes a hybrid creature. It is the origin of the word 'mugger' in Hindi. The Hindi word for Crocodile is (makar, makara). The English word 'mugger' evolved meaning one who sneaks up and attacks another. The name is applied to-the Mugger crocodile, the most common crocodile in India, and is descriptive of its aggressive feeding behavior.

Reference: Vik - 4.54, Kumāra - 14.9

Mālati (मालति)

Meaning/ Scientific term: Flower (*Jasminum grandiflorum*)

Description: Malati is a vine with very fragrant white jasmine-like flowers. This flower is frequently confused with jasmine. Ancient Hindu mythological stories are full of references to Malati flowers, as in the braids of women, or in overhanging bowers under which lovers meet, Malati flowers routinely drop from the hair of women.

Reference: Megha - 40, Ṛtu - 2.25, 3.2, 19

Malaya/Malayamaruta (Kampita) (मलय / मलयमरुत)

Meaning/ Scientific term: Anabatic wind

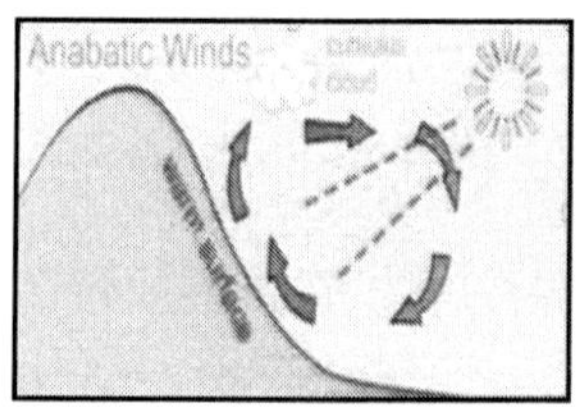

Description: Also called upshore wind, local air current that blows up a hill or mountain slope facing the sun during the day, the sun heals such a slope (and the air over it) faster that it does the adjacent lowland because the slope's surface is more nearly perpendicular to the Sun's rays. This warning decreases the density of the air, causing it to rise. More air rises from below to replace it, producing a wind. An arobatic wind may attain a velocity of 6 metres per sec (about 13 miles per hour).

Reference: Raghu - 9.33, 12.32, 4.46, 51, 6.64, 13.2, Mālā - 3.9, Vik - 3.10, Ṛtu - 6.37, 38, Kumāra - 8.25, Vik - 2.6

Mallikā (मल्लिका)

Meaning/ Scientific term: Flower

Description: Jasminum sambac *Jasminum grandiflorum*, also known variously as the Arabian Jasmine, Spanish jasmine, Royal jasmine, Catalonian jasmine, among other (chameli in Hindi) is a species of jasmine native to South Asia. In India, its leaves are widely used as an Ayurvedic herbal medicine and its flowers are used to adorn the coiffure of women. In Pakistan, it grows wild in the Salt Range and Rawalpindi district at 500-1500 m altitude. It is closely related to, and sometimes treated as merely a form of, Jasminum officinale.

It is widely cultivated as an ornamental plant in warm temperate and subtropical regions.

By method of solvent extraction the Jasmine flowers are converted into Jasmine Concrete and Jasmine Oleoresin (sold as Jasmine Absolute). Both products have a huge demand in the fragrance industry.

Methyl jasmonate isolated from thc jasmine oil of *Jusinum gradiflorum* led to the discovery of the molecular structure of the jasmonate plant hormones.

Reference: Raghu - 16.47, 50

Mandākini (मन्दाकिनी)

Meaning/ Scientific term: Holy River

Description: Name of a holv river. It is a tributary of the Alakananda River. Mandakim originates from the Charabari Glacier near Kedarnath in Uttarakhand, India. The prefix 'mand' (Sanskrit) means "calass" and unhurried, and Mandakini thus signifies "she who flows cleanly".

The Mandakini is mentioned as one of the transcendental river in the holy religious work 'Srimad Bhāgavatam'.

Reference: Kumāra - 3.65

Maṇi/Ratna (मणि / रत्न)

Meaning/ Scientific term: Gemstone

Description: A gemstone or gem (also called a precious or semi-precious stone, or jewel) is a piece of mineral, which, in cut and polished form, is used to make jewelry or other adornments. However certain rocks, (such as lapis lazuli) and organic materials (such as amber or jet) are not minerals, but are still used for jewelry, and are therefore often considered to be gemstones as well. Most gemstones are hard, but some soft minerals are used in jewelry because of their lustre or other physical properties that have aesthetic value. Rarity is another characteristic that lends value to a gemstone.

Reference: Raghu - 1.4, 6.49, 10.7, 10.75, 11.59, 12.65, 13.12, 13.59, 18.42, Mālā - 5.18, Vik - 4.63, 5.2, 5.3, 5.4, 5.5, 5.13, Abhi - 3.11, 7, Ṛtu - 6.4, Nalo - 1.5, 1.18, 3.50, Śṛngāraṣṭakam - 3, Puṣpavānavilāsa - 5.15

Maniśilā (मणिशिला)

Meaning/ Scientific term: Arsenic Sulphate

Reference: Vik - 2, Abhi - 6

Manjari (मन्जरि)

Meaning/ Scientific term: Bud of the flower

Description: In Botany, bud of a flower is an undeveloped or embryonic shoot and normally occurs in the axil of a leaf or at the tip of the stem. Once formed, a bud may remain for sometime in a dormant condition, or it may form a shoot immediately.

Reference: Raghu - 9.44, Vik - 2.7, Abhi - 5.1, Ṛtu - 2.21, 6.20, Śṛngāratilakam - 24

Marakat (मरकत)

Meaning/ Scientific term: Jewel/emerald

Description: Emerald is a variety of the mineral beryl [$Be_3AI_2(Sio_3)_6$] colored green by trace amounts of chromium and sometimes vanadium. Most emeralds are highly included, so their toughness (resistance to breakage) is classified as generally poor. Emeralds, like all .colored gemstones, are graded using four basic parameters - the four Cs of Connoisseurship: Color, Cut, Clarity and Crystal. The last C, crystal is simply used as a synonym that begins with C for transparency or what gemologists call diaphaneity. Normally, in the grading of colored gemstones, color is by far the most important criterion. However, in the grading of emerald, crystal is considered a close second. Both are necessary conditions. A fine emerald must possess not only a pure verdant green hue as described below, but also a high degree of transparency to be considered a top gem.

Reference: Megha - 15, Ṛtu - 3.21

Marubhumi/Maru (मरुभुमि / मरु)

Meaning/ Scientific term: Desert/Sand area absence of soil or natural vegetation

Description: A desert is a landscape or region that receives an extremely low amount of precipitation, less than enough to support growth of most plants. Desert are defined as areas with an average annual precipitation of less than 250m per year, or as areas where more water is lost by evapotransperation that falls as precipitation. The largest .hot desert is the 'Sahara' in northern Africa, covering 9 million sq. km. and 12 countries.

Mineral resources:

Deserts may contain great, amounts of mineral resources over their entire surface. This occurrence in minerals also determines the colour. For example red colour of many sand deserts is a result of the occurrence of laterite. Deserts are increasingly seen as sources for solar energy also.

Reference: Nalo - 1.18, 3.34

Marut (मरुत)

Meaning/ Scientific term: Air

Description: The air or atmosphere of Earth is a mixture of gases surrounding the planet Earth that is retained by Earth's gravity. The air is mainly composed of nitrogen (78%), oxygen (21%), and argon (0.93%) which together constitutes the major gases of the atmosphere and carbon-di-oxide (0.038%). Air also contains a variable amount of water vapor on around 1%, near sea or river side.

Reference: Raghu - 2.10, 2.12, 4.73, 5.27, 7.54, 8.19, 8.32, 8.34, 10.48, 11.3, 12.60, 12.78, 12.101, 16.71, Mālā - 3.4, Abhi - 3, 7.1, Vik - 1.16, 2.17, 5.23, Puṣpavānavilāsa - 13

Matsya (मतस्य)

Meaning/ Scientific term: Fish

Description: A fish is a creature that lives in water and has a tail and fins. There are many different kinds of fish.

Reference: Raghu - 7.40, Abhi - 6

Mauli (मौलि)

Meaning/ Scientific term: Moon

Description: The Moon is the Earth's only natural satellite and the tilth largest satellite in the solar system. The average distance (centre to centre) from the Earth to the Moon is 384, 403 km. which is about thirty times the diameter of Earth. The Moon makes a complete orbit around the Earth every 27.3 days the orbital period and the periodical variations in the geometry of the Earth, Moon, Sun system are responsible for the phase of the Moon, which repeat every 29.5 day.

Reference: Raghu 7.66, 13.51, 59, 17.23, 18.41, Vik - 5

Mayukha (मयुख)

Meaning/ Scientific term: Ray, or beam of light

Description: Rays of light are narrow beams of light.

A beam is a line of energy, radiation or particles sent in a particular direction.

A beam of light is a lime of light that shines from an object such as lamp.

Reference: Kumāra - 3.47, 3.65, Raghu - 16.69, Abhi - 3.3, Ṛtu -3.25, Puṣpavānavilāsa - 23

Mayur/Kalāpa (मयुर / कलाप)

Meaning/ Scientific term: Peacock, Indian Pecock, *Pavo cristatus*

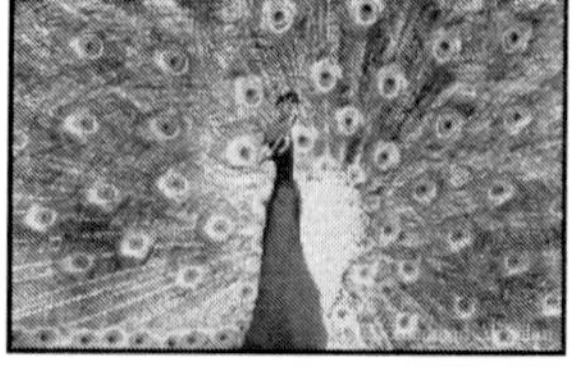

Description: The term "peacock" is commonly used to refer to birds of both sexes. Technically, only males are peacocks. Females are peahens, and together, they are called peafowl.

Peacocks are large, colorful pheasants (typically blue and green) known for their iridescent tails. These tail feathers, or coverts, spread out in a distinctive train that is more than 60 percent of the bird's total body length and boast colorful "eye" markings of blue, gold, red, and other hues. The large train is used in mating rituals and courtship displays: It can be arched into a magnificent fan that reaches across the bird's back and touches the ground on either side. Females are believed to choose their mates according to the size, color, and quality of these outrageous feather trains. Peacocks are ground-feeders that eat insects, plants, and small creatures. There are two familiar peacock species. The blue peacock lives in India and Sri Lanka, while the green peacock is found in Java and Myanmar (Burma).

Reference: Ṛtu - 1.16, 3.12, 20, Raghu - 3.56, 7.69, 9.67, 14.69, 16.14, Mālā - 1.21

Medini (मेदिनि)

Meaning/ Scientific term: Earth

Description: The term earth may merely imply the surface configuration with distinctive form characteristics which can be attributed to the dominance of particular process or particular structures in the course of its development.

Reference: Raghu - 1.65, 9.10, 19.3, Abhi - 7.8

Megha (मेघ)

Meaning/ Scientific term: Cloud

Description: *See* Ambhasa

Reference: Raghu - 12.79, 13.38, 14.8, 15.58, 18.38, 19.39, Mālā - 3.21

Meru (मेरु)

Meaning/ Scientific term: Two Poles of earth; North pole and South pole

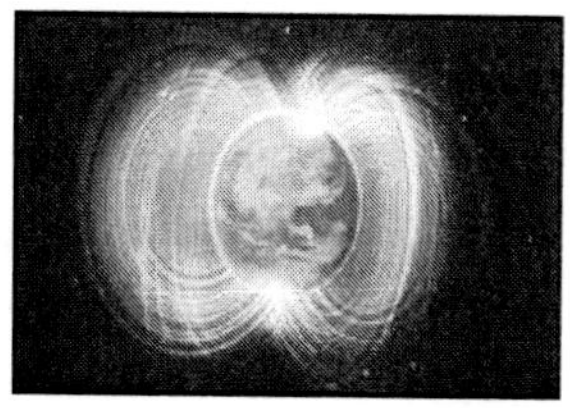

Description: The Earth's poles are the too opposite ends of its axes, its most northera and southerapoints. South pole is the placed on the surface of the earth which is farthest tower and the south. North pole is the place on the surface of the earth which is farthest tower of the north.

Reference: Kumāra - 1.2, 18, 7.79, 8.22, Raghu - 17.26, 7.24

Mohanā (मोहना)

Meaning/ Scientific term: Bay

Description: Bay is a broad curved inlet of the sea, where river usually meets the sea.

Reference: Vik - 1.9

Mṛdanga (मृदंग)

Meaning/ Scientific term: Musical Instrument

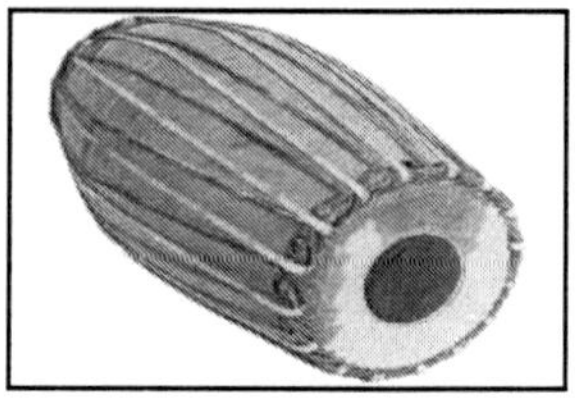

Description: The alternate spellings include "mridanga", "mrdangam" etc. The mridangam is a, percussion instrument from India especially south India. It is the primary rhythmic accompaniment in a carnatic music ensemble. The word "mridangam" is derived from the two Sanskrit words "Mrid" (i.e., clay or earth) and "ang" (body). Early mridangam were indeed made of hardened clay. Over the years, the mridangam evolved to be made of different kinds of wood due to its increased durability, and today its body is constructed from wood of the jackfruit tree.

In ancient Hindu sculpture, painting, and mythology the mridangam is offen depicted as the instrument of choice for a number of deities including Ganesha and Nandi. Nandi, who is the vehicle and companion of Lord Shiva have played the mridangam daring shiva's Tandava dance, causing a derive rhythim to resound aero the hearnens. The mridangam is thus also known as Instrument of the Gods.

Reference: Raghu - 13.40, 16.13, 14, 64, 19.5, Mālā - 1

Mṛga/Hariṇa (मृग / हरिण)

Meaning/ Scientific term: Deer, Cheetal, *Axis axis*

Description: A deer is a large wild mammal that eats grass and leaves. A male deer usually has large, branching horns.

Reference: Kumāra - 1.15, Abhi - 6.16, 6.17, Raghu - 6.3, 9.21, 11.23, 2.53, 11, 17, 30, 43, 18.7, 35, Ṛtu - 1.11, 14, 25, 27, 4.8, Abhi - 1.8, 4.12, Kumāra - 9.25, 14.10, 15.41, 8.38, Vik - 4.8, 59, Raghu - 1.40, 50, 52, 4.74, 5.7, 9, 21, 50, 53, 55, 58, 64, Śṛngāratilakam - 14, 16, Puṣpāvānavilāsa - 18

Mrganabhi (मृगनाभि)

THE MUSK

Meaning/ Scientific term: Musk deer (*Moschus*)

Description: It is a strong-smelling secretion produced by the glands of Asia's musk deer, (i.e., Kastur Mriga) has been used in perfumes and the traditional medicine of China and its neighbours for 5000 years or more.

Reference: Raghu - 17.24

Mrinal (मृनाल)

Meaning/ Scientific term: Lotus

Description: *See* Abja

Reference: Ṛtu 1.19, Raghu - 16.7, 16, Kumāra - 1.40, 3.49, 5.29, 6.68, Vik - 1.20, 5, 3.13, Abhi - 3, 6.18, Śṛngāratilakam-1

Mṛtpātra (मृतपात्र)

Meaning/ Scientific term: Earthen pot

Description: Pot made of earth i.e., soil and clay. Pot or bowl or vases which made in a pottery and shaped from moist clay and hardened by heat.

Reference: Raghu - 6.76

Mṛttika (मृत्तिका)

Meaning/ Scientific term: Earth/Soil

Description: Soil is the substance on the surface of the earth in which plants grow. From surface 0 to 15 cm can consider as soil mass.

Reference: Abhi - 4, 7

Muktā/Múktāphala (मुक्ता / मुक्ताफल)

Meaning/ Scientific term: Pearl /Jewel

Description: A Pearl is produced within the soft tissuss, specifically the martle of a living shelled mollusk. Just like the shell of a mollusk, a pearl is made up of Calcium Carbonate (CaC03) in minute crystathime form, which has been deposited in concentric layer. The first quality naturals have been lightly valued as gemstones and objects of beauty for many countries. The word pearl has become a metaphor for something very rare, fire, admirable and valuable.

Hindu Scriptures:

The Vedic tradition describes the sacred Nine Pearls which were first documented in the Garuda Purāna and one of the books of the Hindu holy text Atharvaveda. Ayurveda contrary reference to pearl ponders as a stimulant of digestion and to treat mental ailments.

Reference: Kumāra - 1.42, 3.53, Raghu - 17.23, Megha (Uttara) 49, Raghu - 13.17, 13.54, 16.18, 69, Ṛtu - 6.8, Puṣpavānavilāsa - 10, 11 Kumāra - 1.6, 6.10, 9.24, Raghu-6.28, 16.62, 67, Mālā, (Viskambhaka Part)

N

Nabha/Niśitha (नभ / निशीथ)

Meaning/ Scientific term: Sky

Description: The sky is the part of the atmosphere or of outer space visible from the surface of any astronomical objects. During day time the sky of earth has the appearance of a deep surface because of the airs scattering of sunlight. The sky is sometimes defined as the denser gaseous use of a planet's atmosphere. At night the sky has the appearance of a black surface or region scattered with stars.

Reference: Raghu - 4.8, 8.15, 17.41, 18.6, Megha - 69, Ṛtu - 3.5, 10, 12, Nalo - 2.19

Nāḍi (नाड़ी)

Meaning/ Scientific term: Pulse

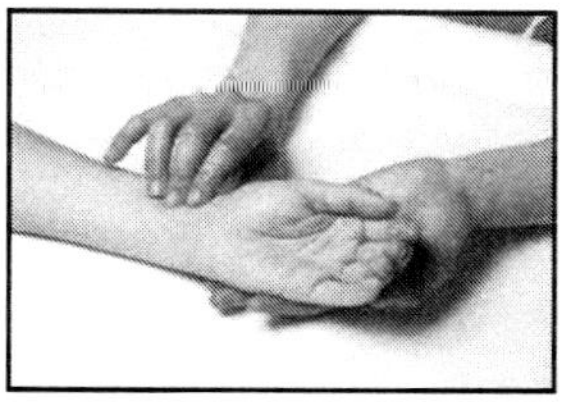

Description: According to medical science, pulse represents the tactile arterial palpation of the heartbeat. The pulse may be palpated in any place that attons an artery to be compressed against a bone, such as at the neck (carotid artery), at the wrist (radial artery), below the knee (portiteal artery), on the inside of the elbow (bractial artery), and near the ankle joint (posterior tibial artery). The pulse rate can also be measured by measuring the heart beat directly (auscultation), usually using a stethoscope.

A normal pulse rate for a healthy adult, while resting, our range from 60 to 100 beats per minute (BPM) which means that the heart is stowel down because there is no activity which require a light heart rate.

Reference: Raghu - 10.58

Nakṣatra/Tārā (नक्षत्र / तारा)

Meaning/ Scientific term: Star, Stella

Description: A star is a massive, luminous ball of plasma that is held together by gravity. The nearest star to Earth is the Sun which is the source of most of the energy on Earth. Other stars are visible in the night sky when they are not outshowed one by the Sun for most of its life, a star shines due to thermonuclear fusion in its care releasing energy that traverses the star's interior and them radiates into outer space. A star begins as a collapsing cloud of material composed primarily of hydrogen, along with helium and trase amounts of lavier elements. Once the stellard core is sufficiently dense, some of the hydrogen is steadilly converted into helium through the process of nuclear fusion.

Reference: Raghu - 6.66, Mālā - 4

Nalini (नलिनी)

Meaning/ Scientific term: Lotus

Description: *See* Abja

Reference: Raghu - 6.44, 8.45, Vik - 4.20, Abhi - 3, 3.20, 24, Ṛtu - 2.14, 3.10, Kumāra - 4.6, Nalo - 2.43, Śṛngāratilakam - 7

Nayan (नयन)

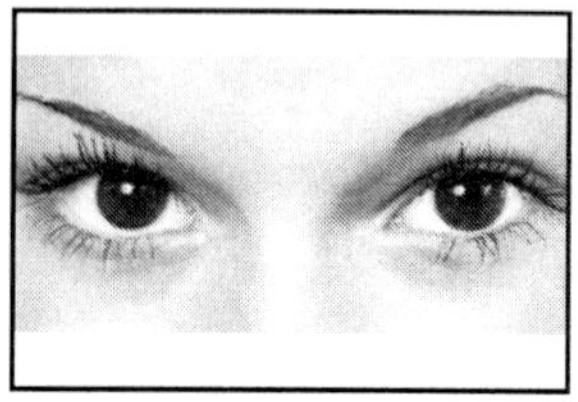

Meaning/ Scientific term: Eye

Description: See Locana

Reference: Abhi 4.15, Śṛngāratilakam - 7, 18, Śrangāraṣṭakam - 2, Puṣpavānavilāsa - 1, 3, 4, 11, 26

Netra (नेत्र)

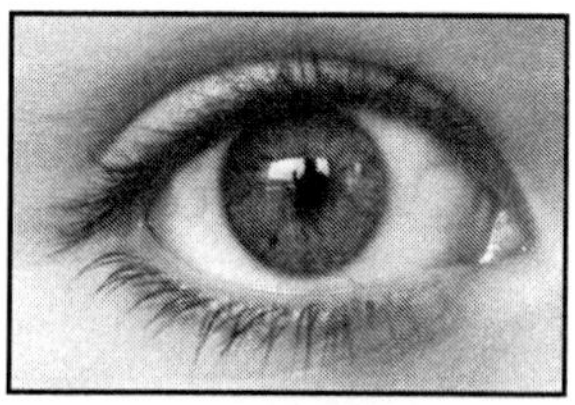

Meaning/ Scientific term: Eye

Description: See Locana

Netravivar (नेत्रविवर)

Meaning/ Scientific term: Eyehole

Description: Eye sockets are the two hollow parts on either side of our face, where our eyeballs are.

Reference: Raghu - 9.61

Nipa (नीप)

Meaning/ Scientific term: Tree

Reference: Raghu - 19.37, Megha - 22

Niśā/Niśi (निशा / निशि)

Meaning/ Scientific term: Night

Description: The period between sunset and sunrise, especially the hours of darkness. The period of darkness each 24 hours between sunset and sunrise, as distinct from day, absence of light, a place having little or no light.

Reference: Vik - 1.9, 3, 3.7, Ṛtu - 5.7, 10, 14, Śṛngāratilakam - 12

O

Ouṣadhi (औषधि) Medicine

Meaning/ Scientific term: Herbal Medicine. In ancient India treatment was performed using indigenous medicine. The main bulk of indigenous medicines are herbal in nature. The study of history of herbal medicine is very very important study in our country. This is not only for training of physicians but also in reviving, assessing and reconstructing the indigenous system of medicines. A great deal of effort is required to produce and accurate and complete history of these systems of medicine and to evaluate how far the basic principles contained in them.

Description: *See* Mahoisodhi

Reference: Raghu - 2.32, 10.66, 12.78, 12.97, 12.61, 14.80, Abhi - 7

P

Pādapa (पादप)

Meaning/ Scientific term: Tree

Description: A tree is a tall plant with a trunk and branches and roots. Roots are usually under the ground. Trees can live for many years. A tree is a perennial woody plant. It is most often defined as woody plant that has many secondary branches supported clear of the ground on a single main stem or trunk with clear apical dominance. A tree is a plant forms that occur in many different orders and families of plants. Trees show a varity of growth forms, leaf type and shape, bark characterities and reproductar organs.

Reference: Vik - 4.68, Raghu - 2.34, 1.51, 12.3, Abhi - 1, 2, 5.7, Ṛtu - 2.27

Padma (पद्म)

Meaning/ Scientific term: Lotus (Nelumbo nucifera)

Description: *See* Abja

Reference: Kumāra - 11.25, 5.19, 27, 7.16, 38, 8.23, 1.16, 38, 1.43, Raghu - 16.16, 17.23, Ṛtu - 4.1, 14, 3.1, 6.2, 3.15, Raghu - 3.17, 6.26, 36, 86, 9.80, 74, 10.8, 62, 13.51, Śṛngāraṣṭakam - 6

Pāndupatra (पान्डुपत्र)

Meaning/ Scientific term: Pale leaf

Description: Old or aged leaf of a tree, which is not green in colour.

Reference: Raghu - 11.28, Abhi - 5.13

Pāndura/Pāndu (पान्डुर)

Meaning/ Scientific term: Pale

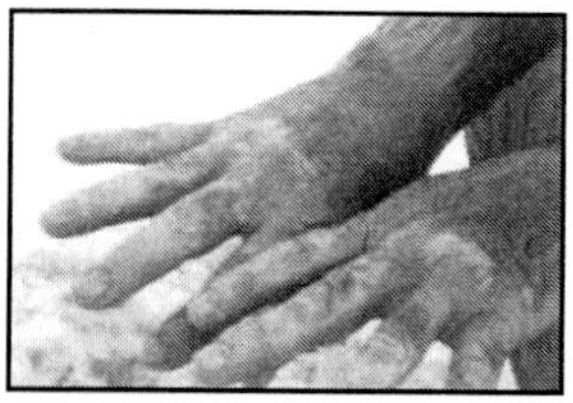

Description: Paleness is an abnormal loss of color from normal skin or mucous membranes.

Reference: Raghu - 10.59, 14.26, 19.50, Mālā - 3.8, Vik - 2.6, 5.8, Abhi - 4.5, 4.12, 6.2, Megha - 18, Ṛtu - 1.9, 2.13, 4.6

Pankaj (पंकज)

Meaning/ Scientific term: Lotus

Description: See Abja

Reference: Abhi - 5.28, 7.16, Ṛtu - 5.5, Śṛngāraṣṭakam - 23

Parabhṛt (परभृत)

Meaning/ Scientific term: Cuckoo/*Ardea cinerea* - Grey heron

Description: A Cuckoo is a bird that has a call of two quick notes, and lays its eggs in other birds nest.

Reference: Mālā - 1, 4, 2, 5.1, Vik - 1.3, 4, Abhi - 4.10, 5.22, 6, Ṛtu - 6.22, Kumāra - 6.2, Raghu - 9.43

Parāg (पराग)

Meaning/ Scientific term: Pollen, Farina

Description: Pollen is a fine to coarse ponders containing the micro gametophytes of seed plants, which produced the male gametes (sperm cells). Pollen graines have a hard coat that perfects the sperm cells during the process of their movement between the stamens to pistil of flowering plants or from the male cone to the female cone of coniferous plants. When pollen lands on a compatible pistil of flowring plants, it germinates and produces pollen.

Reference: Raghu - 16.7, Nalo - 2.30, 2.33, 2.42

Paramāṇu (परमाणु)

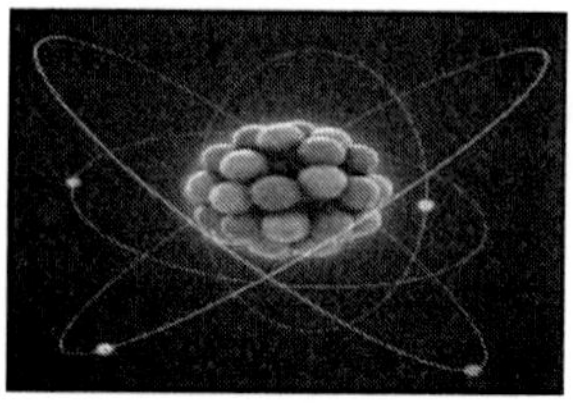

Meaning/ Scientific term: Atom

Description: Atom is the smallest or basic unit of any matter or element consisting of a dense, central nucleus, surrounded by a cloud of negatively charged particles i.e. electrons. Two or a group of atoms can remain bound to each other, forming a molecule. An atom containing an equal number of electrons and protons is electrically neutral, otherwise it has a positive or negative charge and is an own. An atom is classified accessing to the member of protons and neutrons in its nucleus.

Reference: Raghu - 15.22

Pārāvat (पारावत)

Meaning/ Scientific term: Pigeon/*Columbia livia*

Description: Pigeons are gentle, plump, small-billed birds with a skin saddle (cere) between the bill and forehead. All pigeons strut about with a characteristic bobbing of the head. Because of their long wings and powerful flight muscles, they are strong, swift fliers. Pigeons are monogamous; i.e., they mate for life, and the survivor accepts a new mate only slowly. The female lays two glossy white eggs in a flimsy nest that barely holds them. The female generally incubates the eggs by night, the male by day. The incubation period is 14 to 19 days, but the young are cared for in the nest for another 12 to 18 days.

Reference: Mālā - 2.12, Vik - 3.2, Megh - 42

Pārijāta (परिजात)

Meaning/ Scientific term: Flower (*Nyctanthes arbortristis*), oleaceae (gene)

Description: According to mythology, Pārijāta is a heavenly tree brought to earth by lord Krishna. A quarrel over it ensued between Satyabhama and Rukmini, Krishna's wives. Krishna planted the tree in Satyabhama's courtyard in a way but when the tree flowered, the flowers fell in Rukmini's courtyard.

Lord Vishnu's heavenly throne is placed under a flowering Parijata tree, and Hanuman lives under its shade. Another romantic story woven around the tree is about princess Parijata who fell in love with the sun. When he deserted her she committed suicide and a tree sprung from the ashes. Unable to stand the sight of the lover who left her, the tree flowers only at night and sheds them like tear-drops before the sun rises. This flower is also called Siuli.

Reference: Kumāra - 8.27, 9.38, Raghu - 6.6, 10.11, Vik - 2.12

Parṇa (पर्ण)

Meaning/ Scientific term: Leaf

Description: In botany, leaf is an above ground plant organ specialized for photosynthesis. Leaf is the kitchen of a plant. Leaves are also the sites in most plants where transpiration and guttation take place. Leaves can store food and water and modified our some plants for other purpose.

Reference: Raghu - 1.95, 12.40, Abhi - 7.8

Parvat (पर्वत)

Meaning/ Scientific term: Mountain, see Adri

Description: A mountain is a large land form that sketches above the surroundings land in a limited area usually in the form of peak. A mountain is generally steeper than till. Or a natural elevation of the earth surface rising more or less abruptly from the surroundings level and waiting an attitude which, relataty to the adjacent elevation is impressive or movable.

Reference: Kumāra - 1.52, 1.58, Raghu - 6.60, 6.61, 16.70, 17.64, Megha - 14, Nalo - 3.11, Ṛtu - 1.25

Pāvaka (पावक)

Meaning/ Scientific term: Fire

Description: Fire is the rapid oridation of a material in the chemical process of combustion, realeating heat, light and various reaction products. The visible portion of fire is called flame and consists of glowing hot gases. Fire in its most common form can result in conflagration, which has the potential top cause physical damage through burning; Fire has been used by humans for cooking, generating heat, signaling and propulsion purposes.

Reference: Raghu - 3.9, Ṛtu - 1.24

Pavana (पवन)

Meaning/ Scientific term: Air

Description: Air is the mixture of gases which forms the Earth's atmosphere and which we breathe.

Reference: Raghu - 7.43, 11.52, 15.23, 17.64, 19.54, Vik - 2,

Abhi - 3.5, 6.17, Ṛtu - 1.24, 1.25, 1.26, 2.23, 3.15, 6.2, Nalo - 3.17, Raghu - 16.36, Abhi - 4.19

Paya (पय)

Meaning/ Scientific term: Milk

Description: *See* Payas

Reference: Raghu - 5.59, 13.62, Abhi - 7.30

Payas/Payaodhara/Payanidhi/Payoda (पयस्/पयोधर/पयोनिधि/पयोद)

Meaning/ Scientific term: Milk

Description: Milk is a transluceat white liquid produced from the mammary glands of mammals. It contains significant amounts of glurated fat, protein and calcium as well as vitamin C. But the exact components of raw milk vary by speceies to speceies. Cow milk has a pH ranging from 6.4 to 6.8 making it slightly acidic. Milk provides the primary source of nutrition for young infant mammals before they are able to digest other types of food. Payasam is made from boiling milk, rice and sugar. It is very popular in Indian subcontinent and usually offered to Hindu god and goddess.

Reference: Raghu - 2.36, 63, 5.59, 13.14, 13.60, Ṛtu - 2.7, 11, 20, 3.4, 4.3, 5.9, Śṛngarasṭakam - 5

Payomucā (पयोमुचा)

Meaning/ Scientific term: Cloud

Description: A cloud is a visible mass or droplets or little drops of water or frozon crystals suspended in the atmosphere above the surface of the Earth or another planetary body. Clouds are studied in the nephrology or cloud physics branch of meteorology.

Reference: Raghu - 10.61, Ṛtu - 2.10

Peśalam (पेशलम्)

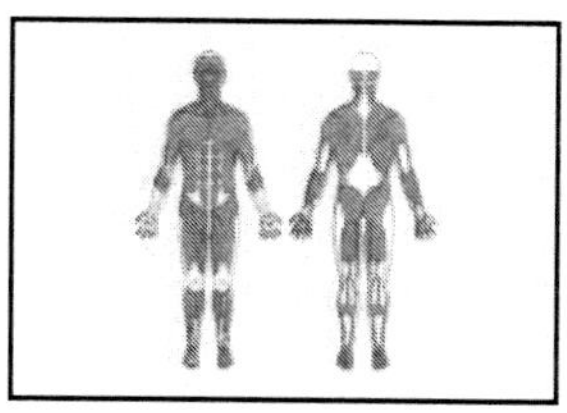

Meaning/ Scientific term: Beautiful, muscular

Description: A muscle is a piece of tissue inside your body which connects two bones and which we use when we want to make a movement.

Reference: Raghu - 9.40

Pitta (पित्त)

Meaning/ Scientific term: Bile

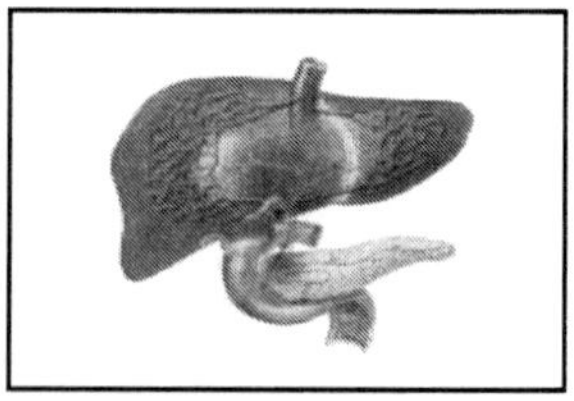

Description: Bile or gall is a bitter-testing dark green to yellow is brown complex fluid containing water electrolytes and a battery of organic power including bile acids, cholesterol, phospholipids and bilirubin that flow through the biliary tract into the small intestine. The two important fundamental functions of bile are (i) bile contains bile acids, which are critical for digestion and absorption of fats and fat-soluble vitamins in the small intestine, (ii) many waste products, including bilirubin are eliminated from the body by secretion into bile and elimination in faeces.

Adult human produce 400 ml to 800 ml of bile daily. In many species, bile is stored in the gall baldder and upon eating is discharged into the duodemem.

Bile aids the process of digestion of lipids in the small intestine.

Reference: Śṛngaratilakam - 15

Prabhāmandala (प्रभामन्डल)

Meaning/ Scientific term: Galaxy, Halo, Cluster of ray

Description: A galaxy is an extremely large group of stars and planets that extends over many billions of light years.

Reference: Kumāra - 1.24, Raghu - 14.14, 15.82, 17.23

Pradipa (प्रदीप)

Meaning/ Scientific term: Lamp

Description: Domestic light source during night-time.

Reference: Raghu - 12.1, 16.4

Prāṇi (प्राणि)

Meaning/ Scientific term: Animal

Description: An animal is living creature such as a dog, lion, or rabbit, rather than a bird, fish, insect or human being.

Reference: Abhi - 5.9, Ṛtu - 2.29

Prasādhan (प्रसाधन)

Meaning/ Scientific term: Cosmetics

Description: Particularly used by the females for make-up, beautification of lady etc.

Reference: Abhi - 6, Mālā - 3.5

Prasravan (प्रस्रवन)

Meaning/ Scientific term: Hot spring

Description: A hot spring is a spring that is produced by the emergence of geothermally heated groundwater from the Earth's crust. There is hot springs all over the Earth, on every continent and even under the oceans and seas. A natural spring with warm water temperature above body temperature - normally between 36.5 °C (97.7 °F) and 37.5 °C (99.5 °F). A natural discharge of groundwater with elevated temperature.

Reference: Ṛtu - 2.16

Pratibimba (प्रतिबिम्ब)

Meaning/ Scientific term: Reflection

Description: Reflection is the change in direction of a wave front at an interface between two different media so that the wavefront returns into the medium from which it originated. Common examples include the reflection of light, sound and water waves. The law of reflection says that for specular reflection the angle at which the wave is incident on the surface equals the angle at which it is relflected. Mirrors exhibit specular reflection.

Laws of reflection

If the reflecting surface is very smooth, the reflection of light that occurs is called specular or regular reflection. The laws of reflection are as follows:

1. The incident ray, the reflected ray and the normal to the reflection surface at the point of the incidence lie in the same plane.
2. The angle which the incident ray makes with the normal is equal to the angle which the reflected ray makes to the same normal.
3. The reflected ray and the incident ray are on the opposite sides of the normal.

Reference: Mālā - 1, Abhi - 6, Ṛtu - 1.4

Pratipa (प्रतिप)

Meaning/ Scientific term: Vertically opposite

Description: Two points or places which are positionally vertically opposite to each other.

Reference: Abhi - 4.18, Raghu - 11.62

Pravāha (प्रवाह)

Meaning/ Scientific term: Wave

Description: A wave is a raised mass of water on the surface of water, especially the sea, which is caused by the wind or by tides making the surface of the water rise and fall.

A wave is a sudden increase in heat or energy that spreads out from an earthquake or explosion.

A wave is a sudden increase in a particular activity or type of behaviours, especially an undesirable or unpleasant air.

Reference: Raghu - 13.10, 16.58, Abhi - 1, 7.6

Pravālam (प्रवालम्)

Meaning/ Scientific term: Coral/*Platygyra lamellina*

Description: Corals are marine organisms from the class Authozoa and exist as small sea amemone - like polyps, typically in colonises of many identical individuals. The group includes the important reef builders that are found in tropical regions, which secrete calcium carbonate to form a hard skeleton.

Reference: Raghu - 7.21, 13.49, 18.52, Ṛtu - 3.18, 4.1, 6.17, Puṣpavānavilāsa - 16

Prayoga vijñanam (प्रयोग विज्ञानम्)

Meaning/ Scientific term: Practical Application of science or scientific knowledge

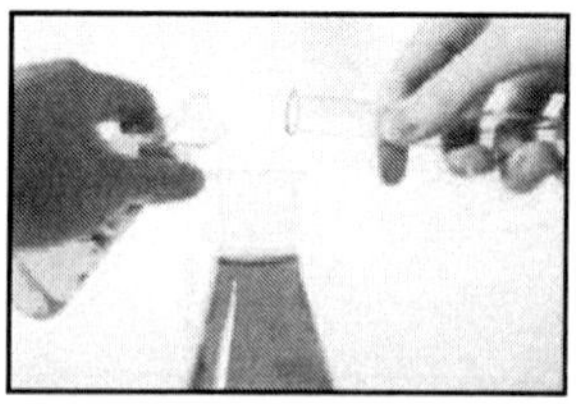

Description: Practical Application of science or scientific knowledge generated in the laboratory of in the university or institute.

Reference: Mālā - 1, 4.5, Abhi - 1.2

Prithvi (पृथ्वी)

Meaning/ Scientific term: Earth

Description: Earth is the planet on which we live. People usually say Earth when they are referring to the planet as part of the universe or of the Solar- system, and the Earth when they are talking about the planet as the place where we live.

Reference: Kumāra 1.1, Mālā - 4, Abhi - 7

Pundarika (पुन्डरीक)

Meaning/ Scientific term: White lotus

Reference: Kumāra - 8.58, Vik - 4.42, Raghu - 4.17, 10.9, 18.8, Mālā - 4.7

Puṣkara (पुष्कर)

Meaning/ Scientific term: Lotus in blue variety Blue lily (*Nymphaea caerulea*) Lotus - *Nelumbo nucifera*

Description: The dark complexion of; Krishna is compared to that of Neelkamal. For this reason, the Blue Waterlily is also called Krishna Kamal. In the 'Ramayana', as it goes, Rama went to 'Lanka' to rescue his abducted wife, Sita, from the grip of Ravana, the king of the Demons in Lanka. Before starting for his battle with Ravana, Rama wanted the blessings of Devi Durga. He came to know that the Goddess would be pleased only if she is worshipped with one hundred 'Neel Kamal' or blue lotuses. Rama, after travelling the whole world, could gather only ninety nine of them. He finally decided to offer one of his eyes, which resembled blue lotuses. Durga, being pleased with the devotion of Rama, appeared before him and blessed him.

Reference: Kumāra - 3.65, Raghu - 18, 30, 31, 37

Puṣpa/Kusum (पुष्प / कुसुम)

Meaning/ Scientific term: Flower

Description: A flower is the part of a plant which is often brightly coloured, grows at the end of a stem, and only survives for a short time and vegetative part of a plant.

Reference: Raghu - 5.52, 10.49, 12.94, 102, 15.8, 20, 16.54, 74, Mālā 3.19, Vik - 4.35, Ṛtu - 3.18, 6.2, 17, Śṛṅgārāṣṭakam - 6, Śṛṅgāratilakam - 11, Puṣpavānavilāsa - 5

Puṣti (पुष्टि)

Meaning/ Scientific term: Nutrition

Description: Nutrition is the process of taking food into the body and absorbing the nutrients in those foods. Nutrition is the science of food. Nutrients and other substances there in, their sciences, interactions and balances in relationship to health and disease. In addition, nutrition is also concerned with socio-economic, cultural and psychological implacents of foods and eating. In short, nutritional science is the area of knowledge regarding the role of food in the maintenance of health.

Reference: Raghu - 18.32

R

Rāgalekhā/Rāga (रागलेखा)

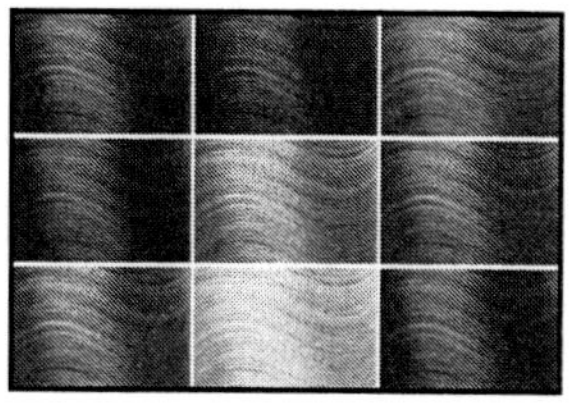

Meaning/ Scientific term: Dye

Description: Natural colour used for colouring the hair, cloth etc.

Reference: Vik - 5.2, Ṛtu - 5.11, Puṣpavānavilāsa - 1

Raja (रज)

Meaning/ Scientific term: Dust

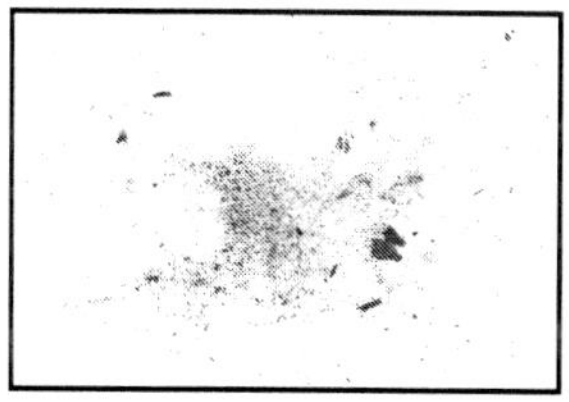

Description: Dust is a general name for minute solid particles with diameters less than 500 micrometers. Dust is very small dry particle of earth or sand. Dust is the very small of dirt which we find inside building, for example on furniture, floors. Dust is a fine powder which consists of very small particles of substance such as gold, wood or coal.

Reference: Raghu - 1.42, 1.85, 7.40, 7.41, 7.42, 7.70, 12.82, 13.64, 15.20, Puṣpavānavilāsa - 1, Mālā - 3.9, Vik - 2.7, 2.19, Abhi - 1.8, 4.11, 6.4, 7.10, 7.17, Ṛtu-2.13, 2.27

Rakta/Rudhira/Rakta Kadamba (रक्त / रुधिर / रक्त कदम्ब)

Meaning/ Scientific term: Blood, the red liquid flowing through the bodies of humans and animals.

Description: See Sonita

Reference: Mālā - 4.4, Vik - 4.33, 34.42, Megha - 76, Raghu - 7.42, 9.23, 12.48, 16.64, 19.64, Mālā - 3.5, Vik - 2.7, Abhi - 4.4, 6, Puṣpavānavilāsa - 7

Rambhā (रम्भा)

Meaning/ Scientific term: Banana

Description: A banana is an edible fruit of the large herbaccous flowering banana plant that belongs to the genes *Musa*.

See Kadali/Kandali

Reference: Mālā - 3.10

Rasa/Rasāyan (रस / रसायन)

Meaning/ Scientific term: Fluid

Description: A fluid is a substance that continiously deforms i.e. flows under an applied shear stress. All gases are fluids, but not all liquids are fluids. Fluids are a subject of the phases of matter and include liquids, gases, plasmas and to some extent, plastic solids. The fluid has the ability to flow that also described any ability to take on the shape of the container. This also means that all fluids have the property of fluidity.

Reference: Mālā - 2.8, Vik - 1.3, Raghu - 1.18, 4.66, 13.3, Ṛtu – 6.35

Rashim (रश्मि)

Meaning/ Scientific term: Ray

Description: *See* Mayukha

Reference: Raghu - 8.29, 11.24, Abhi - 1, 1.8, 3.3

Rāsi (राशि)

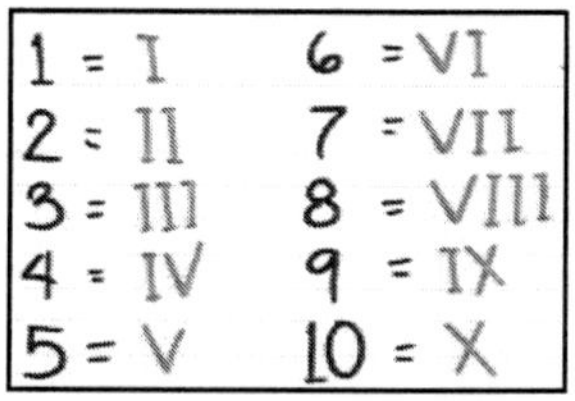

Meaning/ Scientific term: Numerals

Description: Numerals are written symbols used to represent numbers.

Reference: Raghu - 13.53, Mālā - 3

Rātri/Rajani (रात्रि)

Meaning/ Scientific term: Night

Description: *See* Niśā

Reference: Raghu - 16.24, Vik - 1.9, 3.4, Ṛtu - 3.2, 7, 4.15, 5.4, Śṛngārarasṭakam - 2, 5

Rekhā (रेखा)

Meaning/ Scientific term: Line/Straight line

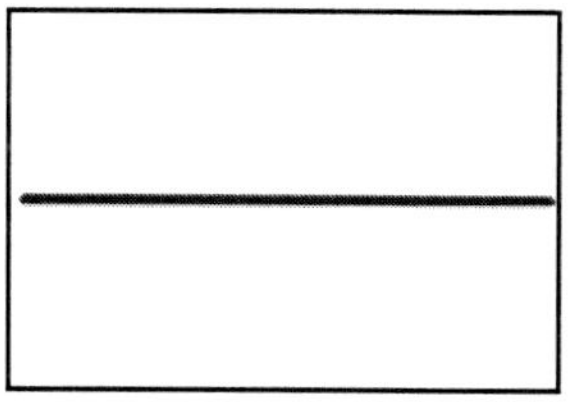

Description: A geometrical object that is straight, infinitely long and infinitely thin. A line is one-dimensional. It has zero width. If you draw a line with a pencil, examination with a microscope would show that the pencil mark has a measurable width. The pencil line is just a way to illustrate the idea on paper. In geometry however, a line has no width. A straight line is the shortest distance between any two points on a plane.

Reference: Raghu - 1.17, 4.88, Abhi - 1.14, 6.14, 6.15

Reṇu/Reṇumanḍala (रेणु / रेणुमन्डल)

Meaning/ Scientific term: Pollen

Description: The fine dust like grains discharged from the male part of a flower, each containing a gamete that can fertilize the female ovule.

Reference: Raghu - 7.39, 43, 9.45, 9.50, 11.11, 13.16, 60, Abhi - 1.30, 4.11, 7.12

Ṛkṣa (रिक्ष)

Meaning/ Scientific term: Bear (*Melursus ursinus*)

Description: A bear is a large and strong wild mammal with thick fur and sharp claws.

Reference: Abhi - 2, Raghu - 13.72

Rohita (रोहित)

Meaning/ Scientific term: A kind of fish freshwater (*Labeo rohita*)

Description: Rohi or Rohu (Labeo rohita, Bengali: Rui) is a fish of the carp family Cyprinidae, found commonly in rivers and freshwater ponds and lakes in and around South Asia and South-East Asia. It is a herbivore. It is treated as a delicacy in Bangladesh and the Indian states of Odisha, Assam, West Bengal, Bihar and Uttar Pradesh. The Kayastha community of Uttar Pradesh treats it as one of their most sacred foods: to be eaten on all auspicious occasions.

In Hindi it is called rehu (rawas is the Indian Salmon, which is quite different). It is called rohi in Oriya, rui in Bengali, Assamese and Sylhet, rohu in Malayalam, and is grown in Kerala in agricultural basis. It is popular in Thailand, Bangladesh, northern India and Pakistan. It is a non-oily/white fish.

Reference: Abhi - 6

Ṛtu (ऋतु)

Meaning/ Scientific term: Season

Description: Each of the four major durations of the year i.e. spring, summer, autumn and winter marked by particular weather and daylight.

Reference: Abhi - 6, Nalo 2.8

Rudra (रुद्र)

Meaning/ Scientific term: Agni (Fire)

Description: Fire is the rapid oridation of a material in the chemical process of combustion, relating heat, light and various reaction products. The visible portion of fire is called flame and consists of glowing hot gases. Fire in its most common form can result in conflagration, which has the potential to cause physical damage through burning. Fire has been used by humans for cooking, generating heat, signaling and propulsion purposes.

Reference: Raghu - 2.54, Nalo - 1.11, 1.51, Śruto - 38

S

Śabda (शब्द)

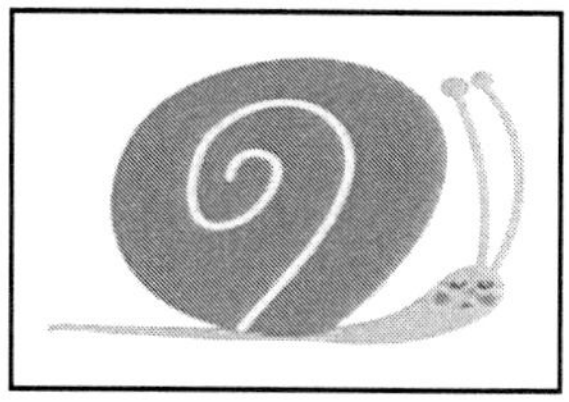

Meaning/ Scientific term: Sound

Description: Sound is basically an energy which travels through a medium.

Reference: Raghu - 2.53, 3.49, 5.22, 11.73, 13.1, 14.4, 18.3, 42, Mālā - 5.16, Vik - 1, 1.3, 2.16

Sāgara (सागर)

Meaning/ Scientific term: Ocean

Description: A sea generally refers to a large body of salt water, but the term is used in other contexts as well. Most commonly, the term refers to a large expanse of saline water connected with an ocean, and is commonly used as a synonymn for ocean. It is also used sometimes to describe a large saline take that lacks a natural outlet, such as the Caspian sea.

Reference: Raghu - 11.75, 12.60, 18.4, Abhi - 3, Nalo - 2.2

Sahakāra (सहकार)

Meaning/ Scientific term: Mango tree (*Mangifera indica*) See Āmrakut/Āmra

Description: A mango is a large sweet yellowish fruit which grows on a tree in hot countries. This is national fruit of India.

Reference: Vik - 2.6, Abhi - 1, 3, Kumāra - 4.38, 8.78, Raghu - 6.69, 8.61, 9.33, 16.52, 19.46, Mālā - 4.13, Nalo - 2.14

Śaibāl (शैबाल)

Meaning/ Scientific term: Moss, Algae is a large diverse group of phytosynthetic organisms.

Description: The Saivala (Vallisneria) is an aquatic plant, which spreads itself over ponds, and interweaves itself with the lotus. The interlacing of its stalks is compared in poetry to braided hair. This is a large group of organisms that include *chlorella*, diatoms, giant kelp.

Reference: Raghu - 5.46, 16.61, Abhi - 1.19, Śṛngaratilakam - 1

Śakti (शक्ति)

Meaning/ Scientific term: Power

Description: In physics the rate of doing work, measured in watts or horse power i.e., capacity or performance of an engine or other device. For other words, energy that is produced by mechanical, electrical or other means, i.e., strength, free or energy.

Reference: Raghu - 4.31, 12.77

Śālidhānya (शालिधान्य)

Meaning/ Scientific term: Lowland Paddy variety

Description: Lowland paddy. Paddy variety which can survive under water logged stress condition.

Reference: Ṛtu - 5.16

Salil (सलिल)

Meaning/ Scientific term: Water (H_2O)

Description: Water is a clear liquid that has no clour or text when it is pure. It falls from clouds as rain and enters rivers and seas. All animals and people need water in order to live.

Reference: Raghu - 13.30, 16.72, 19.2, Ṛtu - 1.28, 2.7, 24, Mālā - 1.11

Sālmali (शाल्मलि)

Meaning/ Scientific term: The Seemul on Silk cotton tree *Bombax ceiba*. Seemul or salmali is a fairly large tree that produces simul cotton.

Description: *Bomban Heptaphyllum or Salmalia Malubarica.*

Reference: Ṛtu - 1.26

Samira (समीर)

Meaning/ Scientific term: Air

Description: Mountain breeze is a cold wind comes from the Mountain that develops over the land near mountains, when air passes over the mountain or over elevated surface, heating of the ground exceeds the heating of the surrounding air at the same altitude above sea level or heating associated thermal low over the terrain and enlancing any thermal lows that would have otherwise existed.

Reference: Raghu - 6.26, 17.56

Samirana (समीरन)

Meaning/ Scientific term: Air

Description: *See* Samira

Reference: Kumāra - 1.8, Ṛtu - 2.17

Saṁkhyā (संख्या)

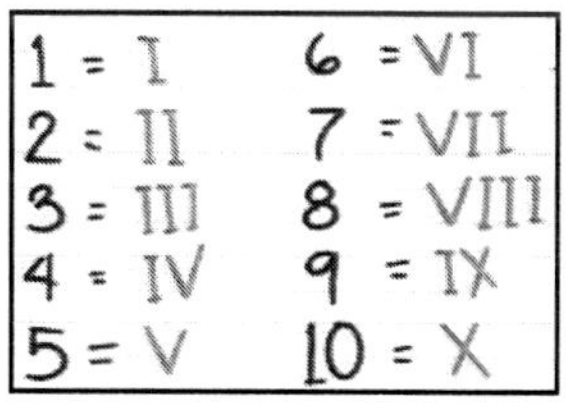

Meaning/ Scientific term: Numeral (1, 2, 3, 4... etc.)

Description: Numerals are written symbols used to represent numbers.

Reference: Raghu - 16.47

Samudra (समुद्र)

Meaning/ Scientific term: Sea

Description: *See* Sagara

Reference: Raghu - 3.28, 4.35, 10.82, 13.11, 14.39, 14.8, 15.83, 16.2, Abhi - 3.18, Mālā - 5.19, Vik - 4, Ṛtu - 1.7, Nalo - 1.29, 2.58

Śaṅkha (शंख)

Meaning/ Scientific term: Conch Shell, Large Indian Shell

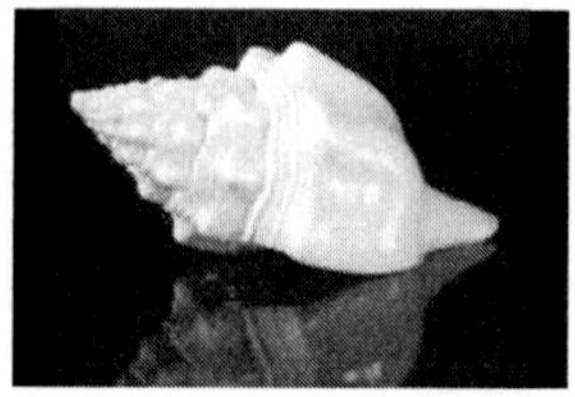

Description: A conch is a common name which is applied to a number of different species of medium-sized to large sea snails or their shells, generally those which are large and have a high spire and a siphonal canal. True conches are marine gastropod molluscs in the family Strombidae, specifically in the genus *Strombus* and other closely related genera such as *Eustrombus*.

A Śaṅkha shell (the shell of a *Turbinella pyrum*, a species in the gastropod family (Turbinellidae) is often referred to in the West as a conch shell, or a chank shell. This shell is used as an important ritual object in Hinduism. The shell is used as a ceremonial trumpet, as part of religious practices, for example Puja.

In the story of Dhruva the divine conch plays a special part. The warriors of ancient India blew conch shells to announce battle, as is described in the beginning of the war of Kurukshetra, in the Mahabharata, the famous Hindu epic. The god of Preservation, Vishnu, is said to hold a special conch, Pānchajanya, that represents life, as it has come out of life-giving waters. Also, the sound of the conch is believed to drive away the evil spirits. The blowing of the counch or "the Shankha" needs a tremendous power and respiratory capacity. Hence, blowing it daily helps keep the lungs healthy.

Reference: Ṛtu - 3.4

Sānu (सानु)

Meaning/ Scientific term: Mountain

Description: A mountain is a large land form that sketches above the surroundings land in a limited area usually in the form of peak. A mountain is generally steeper than till. Or

A natural elevation of the earth surface rising more or less abruptly from the surroundings level and waiting an attitude which, relataty to the adjacent elevation is impressive or movable.

Reference: Raghu - 6.60, Vik - 4, Abhi - 7, Ṛtu - 6.27, Nalo - 3.32

Saphara (शफर)

Meaning/Scientific term: *Cyprinus sophore*. Now it is called *Puntius*

Description: A kind of bright little fish that glistens when darting about in shallow water.

Reference: Megha - 40, Kumāra - 4.39, Ṛtu - 3.3

Saptaparṇa (सप्तपर्ण)

Meaning/ Scientific term: Seven leaved flower (*Alstonia scholaris*)

Description: A tree having seven leaves on a stalk (*Echites scholaris*) Synonyms.

Reference: Abhi - 1, Raghu - 4.23

Śara (शर)

Meaning/ Scientific term: Arrow

Description: A thin weapon with a sharp pointed head, designed to be shot from a bow.

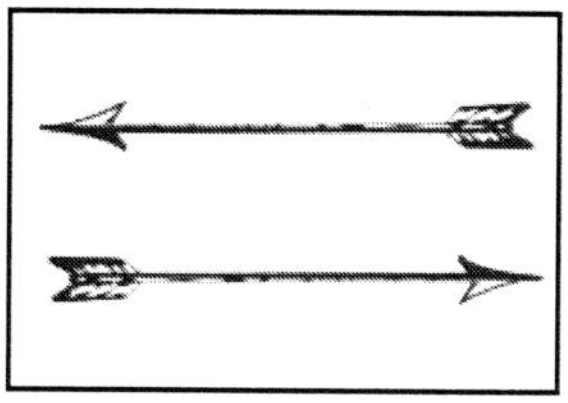

In other word an arrow is a long thin weapon is sharp and pointed at one end and which often has feathers at the other end.

An arrow is a pointed projectile that is shot with a bow. It predates recorded history and is common to most cultures.

Reference: Raghu - 3.56, 9.19, 11.24, 12.78, 12.90, 94, 14.26, Vik - 5, Abhi - 1.7, 3.3, 6.3, 6.4, 6.29, 7.3, Nalo - 2.5

Sara/Saraswati (सर / सरस्वती)

Description: *See* Salil

Reference: Raghu - 11.11, 14.8, Rtu - 1.19, 3.11, 4.9, Nalo-2.39, 2.42, 2.44, Śṛngāratilakam - 1, Puṣpavānavilāsa - 23

Sarala Druma (सरल द्रुम)

Meaning/ Scientific term: Straight tree

Description: Pinus longifolia

Reference: Kumāra 1.9, 2.22, Raghu - 4.75, Megha - 53

Sārasa/Sāranga (सारस / सारंग)

Meaning/ Scientific term: Crane

Description: Antigone. Saras is a large, long legged, and long-necked bird. This bird is a large non migratory crane found in wetlands of Indian subcontinent. The scientific name of Saras is *Antigone*.

Reference: Megha (Purva) - 33, Mālā - 3.1, 3.6, Raghu - 1.41, 13.30, 33, Vik - 4, Abhi - 1.31, Ṛtu - 3.8, 16, Nalo - 2.2, 2.4, 2.10

Sārdula (शार्दुल)

Meaning/ Scientific term: Jackal/*Canis areyas,* Bengal fox = Indian fox Vulpes bengalensis.

Description: A jackal is a wild animal that looks like a dog, has long legs and pointed ears, and lives in Africa and Southern India.

Reference: Abhi - 2, 6.27, Kumāra - 3.44

Śarira (शरीर)

Meaning/ Scientific term: Health/Human body

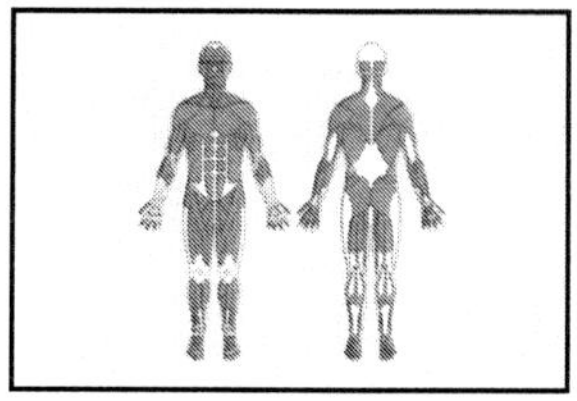

Description: With regards to living things, a body is the physical body of an individual. "Body" offen is used in connection with appearance, health issues and death.

Reference: Raghu - 5.9, 6.65, 8.19, 8.72, 8.87, 8.89, 8.72, 8.89, 13.58, 14.82, 16.23, 18.49, Mālā - 3.1, Vik - 1.20, 2.12, 2.18, 3.11, 3.17, 4, Abhi - 1.32, 3.24, 4, 5.13, 6

Sarit (सरित)

Meaning/ Scientific term: Water

Description: *See* Salil

Reference: Raghu - 4, 24, 5/46/59, 13.48, 14.8, 16.56, 71, Mālā - 3.6, 5.19

Śarja (शर्जा)

Meaning/ Scientific term: A valuable timber tree (*Shorea robusta*)

Description: Sāl is a tall handsome tree providing very good quality timber. Its botanical family is dipterocarpaceae. In local languages it is called salwa, sakhu, sakher, shal kinder and sakwa. It grows well in a well-drained, moist, sandy loam soil. It is a moderate to slow growing species and can attain a height upto 35m and a growth of about 2 to 2.5m in about 100 years under favourable conditions. The body of Sal tree is erect and cylindrical. The bark of the young tree is smooth with a few long deep and vertical furrows. Sal trees are found from Burma in the East, to Assam, Bengal, Nepal, the Decan Plateau, going tp the foothills of the Shivaliks on the left bank of the Yamuna river. Sal growing in Nepal and Singhbhum district of Bihar are considered to be the best variety. Sal tree has a major religious significance. In Hindu tradition the Sal tree is said to be favoured by Visnu. Its name "Shāla", "Shaal" or "Sāl", comes from Sanskrit, other names in the Sanskrit language are Ashavakarna, Chiraparna and Śarja among many others. In Buddhist tradition, it is said that Queen Māyā of Śākya gave birth to Gautam Buddha under a śāl tree or an asoka tree in a garden in Lumbini, in south Nepal while grasping its branch.

Reference: Ṛtu - 3.13, 2.17, Raghu - 1.38

Saroja/Sarasija (सरोज)

Description: *See* Abja

Reference: Abhi - 1.19, Kumāra - 5.27, Mālā - 5.3, Nalo - 2.38, 2.44.

Sarvari (शर्वरी)

Meaning/ Scientific term: Moon

Description: *See* Sasi

Reference: Raghu - 3.2, 8.56, Ṛtu - 2.10

Śaśānka (शशांक)

Meaning/ Scientific term: Moon

Description: *See* Śaśī

Reference: Abhi - 3.15, Ṛtu - 1.2, 5.4, 6.3

Śaśi (शशि)

Meaning/ Scientific term: Moon

Description: The Moon is the Earth's only natural satellite and the fifth largest satellite in the solar system. The average distance (centre to centre) from the Earth to the Moon is 384,403 km., which is about thirty times the diameter of the Earth. The Moon makes a complete orbit around the Earth every 27.3 days (the orbital period), and the periodic variations in the geometry of the Earth-Moon-Sun system are responsible for the phases of the Moon, which repeat every 29.5 days (the synodic period).

The Pull of gravity at its surface is about 17 percent of that at the Earth's surface. The Moon is the only celestial body on which human beings have made a manned landing.

Reference: Raghu - 3.2, 3.16, 6.44/85, 9.7, 11.24, 82, 14.40, 16.27, 53, Vik - 1.9, 3.20, 5.19, Abhi - 7.22, Ṛtu - 12, Nalo - 1.54, 2.52, Śruto - 9, Puṣpavānavilāsa - 15

Śasya (शस्य)

Meaning/ Scientific term: Corn = *Zea mays*

Description: Any of numerous cultivated forms of a widely grown, usually tall cereal grass bearing grains or kernels on large ears. The grains or kernels of this plant, used as food for humans and livestock or for the extraction of an edible oil or starch. Also called *Indian corn, maize*.

Reference: Raghu - 17.66, 18.2

Śatguṇita (शतगुणित)

Meaning/ Scientific term: Hundred (100)

Description: 100 (one hundred) (Roman numeral C, for centum) is the natural number following 99 and preceding 101.

Reference: Vik - 3.22

Ṣaṭpada (षटपद)

Meaning/ Scientific term: Bee

Description: *See* Madhupa

Reference: Raghu - 6.69, 8.55, 9.26, 12.27, Vik - 2.22, 4.21, Śṛngāratilakam - 11, Meghduta - 14, (Uttar Megha)

Savitā (सविता)

Meaning/ Scientific term: Sun

Description: The Sun is only source of our energy. It is the star at the centre of the Solar system and itself accounts for about 99.86% of the Solar system's mass. The Sun's mass consists of hydrogen, while most of the rest is helium. Less than 2% consists of other elements, including iron, oxygen, carbon & neon. Solar energy. Renewable source of energy.

Reference: Raghu - 4.1, 9.50, Vik - 2.1

Śikara (शीकर / सीकर)

Meaning/ Scientific term: Water (H_2O)

Description: *See* Ambha

Reference: Kumāra - 1.15, 2.42, 8.31, Abhi - 7.7, Nalo - 2.53

Śikhandi/Śikhi (शिखन्डि / शिखि)

Meaning/ Scientific term: Peacock

Description: *See* Mayur or Kalāpa

Reference: Kumāra - 1.15, Vik - 5, 13, Ṛtu - 2.14, 16

Śikharini/Śikhi/Śikhanda (शिखरिनी / शिखि / शिखन्ड)

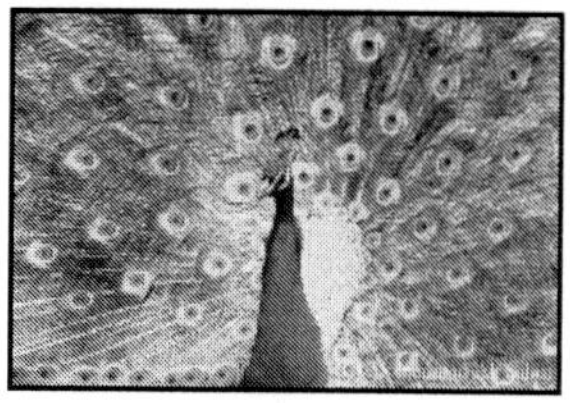

Description: *See* Mayur/Kalpa

Reference: Raghu - 9.17, 13.27, 19.54, Mālā - 2.12, 5.10, Vik - 2.22, 5.13, Abhi - 5, Ṛtu 2.14, 2.16

Śila/Śaila (शिल / शैल)

Meaning/ Scientific term: Stone

Description: The hard non-metalic mineral matter of which rock is made. A gem is a shaped piece of stone designed for particular purpose etc.

Reference: Kumara - 1.2, 1.55, Megha - 12, Raghu - 2.34, 51, 4.51, 4.71, 5.46, 6.3, 11.18, 28, 34, 12.73, 16.26, 49, 18.17, Vik - 1.15, 3.8, Abhi - 2.17, 7.8, Ṛtu - 6.27, Śṛngāratilakam - 1, Śṛngāraṣṭakam - 7

Silimukha (शिलीमुख)

Meaning/ Scientific term: Stone edge

Reference: Raghu - 7.49, 65, 18.17

Sindhu (सिन्धु)

Meaning/ Scientific term: River Sindhu

Description: One of the largest river of Indian Sub-continent will large stream of water flowing over the land.

Reference: Megha - (Purva) - 50, Raghu - 4.35, 13.9, 15.87, Śṛngāraṣṭakam - 7

Sindura (सिन्दुर)

Meaning/ Scientific term: Vermilion/Mercury Sulphide (HgS)

Description: Vermilion sometimes spelled (vermillion), when found naturally occurring is a opaque orangish red pigment used since antiquity, originally derived from the pondered mineral cinualor. Chemically the pigment is mercuric sulfide (Hgs) and like many mercury compounds. It is toxic. Its name is derived from the French vermeil which was used to mean any red dye.

There is evidence of the use of innabar pigment in Spain, China and India since prehistory. In India it is known a Sindoor. The synthesis of vermilia from mercury and sulpher may have bear inverted by the Chinese, the earliest known description of the process dates from the 8th century. The names "cuinabar" and "vermilion" were used interchangeably to describe either the natural or manufactured pigment until the 17th century when vermilion became the more common name, by the late 18th century the name cinnabar was applied only to natural mineral. "China red" is another name for the pigment vermilion, which is the traditional red pigment of Chinese art.

Reference: Ṛtu - 1.24

Śirisha (शिरिष)

Meaning/ Scientific term: Tree

Description: The flower of *Mimosa sirissa*. This is described as a delicate and lovely flower used as an ear-ornament by women.

Reference: Abhi - 6.18, Kumāra - 1.41, 5.4, Raghu - 16.61, 18.45, Abhi - 1.28, 1.4

Śiśira (शिशिर)

Meaning/ Scientific term: Dewdrop

Description: Dew is small drops of water that form on the ground and other surfaces outdoors during the night-time.

Reference: Raghu - 14.3, 16.49, 19.42, Vik - 2.22, Abhi - 3.11, 6.4, 6 Ṛtu - 3.2, Puṣpavānavilāsa - 24

Sonita (शोणित)

Meaning/ Scientific term: Blood, the red liquid flowing through the bodies of humans and animals. The blood cells are mainly red blood cells (also called RBCS or erythrocytes), white blood cells (also called WBCS or leukocytes) and platelets (also called thrombocytes). The most alundant cells in vertebrate blood are red blood cells.

Description: *See* Rudhira, Rakta

Reference: Raghu - 2.39, 3.54, 12.82, 14.41, 7.49

Sphatika (स्फटिक)

Meaning/ Scientific term: Quartz/Crystal

Description: The word "quartz" is derived from the German word "quarz" and its Middle High German ancestor "twarc" which probably originated in Slavic Quartz or sphatika is the second most abundant mineral in the Earth's continental crust. It is made up a continuous framework of Si04 silicon-oxygen tetrahedral, with each oxygen being shared between two tetrahedral, giving an overall formula SiO2.

There are many different varieties of quartz, several of which are semi-precious gemstones. Especially in Europe and the Middle East, varieties of quartz have been antiquity the most commonly used minerals in the making of jewelry and hardstone carvings.

Some macrocrystalline (large crystal) varieties are well known and popular as ornamental stone and as gemstones. Amethyst is the purple gemstone variety.

Citrine is a yellow to orange gemstone variety that is rare in nature but is often created by heating Amethyst.

Milky Quartz is the cloudy white variety.

Prasiolite is a leek-green gemstone variety that is rare in nature but is created by heating Amethyst from certain locations.

Rock crystal is the clear variety that is also used as a gemstone.

Rose quartz is a pink to reddish pink variety.

Smoky quartz is the brown to gray variety.

Reference: Raghu - 13.69, Kumāra - 6.42, 9.40, 9.41, 9.43, 9.46, Megha - (Purva) - 55, Mālā - 4, Vik - 3

Sphulinga/Sphuta (स्फुलिंग)

Meaning/ Scientific term: Fire

Reference: Abhi - 7.15, Nalo - 4.22

Staṁbha (स्तम्भ)

Meaning/ Scientific term: Pillar

Description: A Pillar is similar to a column which is a vertical support structure, but the base section is any shape but circular. A pillar or column in structural engineering is a vertical structural element that transmits, through compressions the weight of the structure above to other structural element below. Pillars are frequently used to support beams or arches on which the upper parts of walls or ceilings nest.

Reference: Raghu - 16.17, 41, 17.9

Stanyapāyī (स्तन्यपायी)

Meaning/ Scientific term: Mammal

Description: Mammals are animals such as humans, dogs, lions, and whales. In general, female mammals give birth to babies rather than laying eggs, and feed their young with milk from mammary gland. Mammals are a group of animal that feed their young with milk from mammary glands. Humans, dogs, cats, lions, whates etc. are examples of mammals

Reference: Raghu - 10.78

Sthala (स्थल)

Meaning/ Scientific term: Earth/Land mass

Description: Land mass

Reference: Raghu - 4.60, 6.64, Nala - 1.41, Kumāra - 1.33, Ṛtu - 4.7

Sthānu (स्थानु)

Meaning/ Scientific term: Land mass

Description: Land is an area of ground, especially one that is used for particular purpose such as farming or building.

Reference: Kumāra - 3.17, 3.34, 8.13, Raghu - 11.13, 14.38, Abhi - 7.11

Sthavira (स्थविर)

Meaning/ Scientific term: Immovable object

Description: Immovable property is an immovable object, an item of property that cannot be moved.

Reference: Kumāra - 3.52, 6.73, 6.80

Surya (सूर्य)

Meaning/ Scientific term: Sun

Description: The sun is a star and the only source of our energy. Renewable source of energy. Solar energy – it is the star at the centre of the Solar system and itself accounts for about 99.86% of the Solar system's mass. The Sun's mass consists of hydrogen, while most of the rest is helium. Less than 2% consists of other elements, including iron, oxygen, carbon and neon.

Reference: Raghu - 3.13, Vik - 5.20

Surya/Savitā/Ravi (सूर्य / सविता / रवि)

Meaning/ Scientific term: Sun

Description: *See* Surya

Reference: Raghu - 5.13, 7.39, 13.12, 14.66, 16.11, 17.26, 17.74, 17.75, Mālā - 4, Vik - 1, 3, 4, 5.20, Abhi - 2.7, 4, Ṛtu - 1.17, 20, 4.15, 5.15, Nalo - 1.33, 2.5

Suryakānta (सूर्यकान्त)

Meaning/ Scientific term: Jewel

Description: Pure quartz, traditionally called rock crystal (sometimes called clear quartz). This is colourless and transparent (clear) or translucent, and has often been used for hardstone carving such as the Lothair Crystal.

Reference: Raghu - 11.21

Suvarna/Gold (सुवर्ण)

Meaning/ Scientific term: See Kānchana/Hema

Description: *See* Kancana/Hema

Reference: Raghu - 3.64

Swapna (स्वप्न)

Meaning/ Scientific term: Dream

Description: A dream is a succession of thoughts, sounds or emotions which the mind experience during sleep. The content and purpose of dreams are not fully understood, though they have been a topic of speculation and interest throughout recorded history. The scientific study of dreams is known as oneirology. Dreams have been described physiologically as a response to neural proceses during sleep, psychologically as reflections of the subconscious and spiritually as masseages from gods, the deceased, or predictions of the future. According to Psychosomatic theory, dreams are a product of "dissociation imagination", which is dissociated from the conscions self and draws materials from sensory memory for simulation, with sensory feed back resulting in hallucination.

Reference: Abhi - 6.10, 6.22

Swedavindu (स्वेदविन्दु)

Meaning/ Scientific term: Sweat

Description: Sweating or perspiration or transpiration or diaploreises is the production of fluid consisting primary of water as well as various dissolved solids (chiefly chloride), that is exracted by the sweat glands in the skin of mammals.

Sweat contains the chemicals or adorants 2-methylphenol (o-cresol) and 4-metheylphenol (P-cresol), as well as a small amount of area.

Reference: Abhi - 6

T

Taila (तेल)

Meaning/ Scientific term: Oil (*oleum*)

Description: Oil is any substance, that is liquid at ambient temperature and is hydrophobic but soluble in organic solvent. Oils have carbon and hydrogen content and are non-polar substances. The general definition above includes vegetable oils, petrochemical oils and volatile essential oils. All oils can be traced back to organic sources. Here we like to mention the essential oil in particular and which is a concentrated, hydrophobic liquid containing volatile aroma compound from plants. Oil, can be resulted from pressing the seeds of a plant, from grinding the seeds (mustered oil), mixing them with water, and extracting the resulting volatile oil by distillation. Oils have been used throughout history as a fragrant or religious medium. Oil is often seen as a spiritually purifying agent. It is used in used in religious ceremonies. Oil that is associated with one or more saint is known as "oil of saints" and believed by some to have beneficial properties, as is "oil of martyrs". Oils are of different types. Essentials oils, Mineral oils, Organic oils, Synthetic oils, Vegetable oils, Petrochemical oils etc.

Reference: Raghu - 8.38

Tālivana/Tāla druma (तालिवन / तालद्रुम)

Meaning/ Scientific term: Tal forest (Asian palmysa palm *Borasous flabellier*)

Description: Palms is a species of palm, native to India (Malabar Coast) and Sri Lanka.

It is one of the largest palms in the world; individual specimens have reached heights of up to 25 m, with stems up to 1.3m in diameter. It is a fan palm (Arecaceae tribe Corypheae), with large palmate leaves up to 5 m in diameter, with a petiole up to 4 m, and up to 130 leaflets. The Talipot palm bears the largest inflorescence of any plant, 6-8 m long, consisting of one to several million small flowers borne on a branched stalk that forms at the top of the trunk, the Titan Arum (Amorphophallus titanum), from the family

Araceae, has the largest unbranched inflorescence, and the species Rafflesia arnoldii has the world's largest single flower. The Talipot palm is monocarpic, flowering only once, when it is 30 to 80 years old. It takes about a year for the fruit to mature, producing thousands of round yellow-green fruit 3-4 cm diameter, containing a single seed. The plant dies after fruiting.

The Talipot palm is originally from India. One of the tallest and most impressive palms with its huge trunk, up to 3 feet in diameter; it grows to a height of 100 feet (34 m) and has very large fan leaves; up to 21 feet (7 m) across. This palm has an enormous inflorescence high above the crown, shaped like an umbrella. The tree produces millions of flowers during it one an only flowering season. The Talipot has round dark-green fruits falling by the thousands when ripe. It grows slowly and lives between 40-80 years. The Talipot is monocarpic, fruits only once during its lifetime; after fruiting it dies. It takes about a year for the fruit to ripen. The seeds are large and germinate easy. Due to its size the tree is only suitable for large tropical parks. Indoors they can be grown in containers for some time but eventually must be moved outdoors.

Reference: Raghu - 6.57, 13.15

Tama (तम)

Meaning/ Scientific term: Dark/Darkness

Description: Darkness is the absence of light, also called lightlessness. A dark object reflects all the light photons than other objects, and therefore appears dim in comiparisa.

Reference: Raghu - 5.71, 13.4, Mālā- 1.9, Vik-3.7, Abhi-6.8, 7.22

Tamāla (तमाल)

Meaning/ Scientific term: Tamāla Tree

Description: Dark-barked but white blossomed. This is represented as growing on senside.

Reference: Raghu - 6.64, 13.15, 13.49, Nalo - 2.37

Tamasa (तमस)

Meaning/ Scientific term: Darkness

Description: Darkness is the absence of light, also called lightlessness. A dark object reflects all the light photons than other objects, and therefore appears dim in comparison.

Reference: Raghu - 9.20, 9.72, 14.76, Vik - 1.9

Tāmbula (तामबुल)

Meaning/ Scientific term: Betel leaf

Description: The Betel (*Piper betle*) is the leaf of a vine belonging to the Piperacae family, which includes pepper and kava. It is valued both as a mild stimulant and for its medicinal properties. The betel plant is an evergreen and perenial creeper, with glossy heart-shaped and white catkin. The betel plant originated from South and South East Asia i.e., India, Bangladesh and Sri Lanka.

The betel plant is a slender, aromatic creeper, nothing at the nodes. The branches of the plants are swollen at the nodes. The plant has alternate, heart-shaped, smooth, shining. and long stalked leaves, with pointed apex. It has five to seven ribs arising'from the base; minute flowers and one-seeded spherical small berries. Betel leaf consist of moisture 85.4%, protein 31%, fat 0.8%, minerals 2.3%, fibre 2.3% and carbohydrates 6.1% per 100 grams. Its minerals and vitamin contents are calcium, carotene, riboflarin, niacin, thyiamine and vitamin c. Recent studies have shown that betel leaves contains tannins, sugar and diastases and an essential oil. The essential Oil is a light yellow liquid of aromatic odor and sharp burning in paste. It contains a phenol called chavicol which has powerful antiseptic properties. The alkaloid arakene in it has properties resembling cocaine in some respects.

Use of Betel leaves:

The betel leaves are chewed together with betel nut as a masticatory. In its simplest form, sliced betel nut is wrapped in a betel leaf, sweared with lime and chewed. Often through a clove and other spices such as cuinaneow and cardamom are added. When chewed after meals, it sweetens the breath and acts as a gentle stimulant. Health benefits of Betel leaves:

Health benefits of Betel leaves:

(i) The betel leaf has analgesic and cooling properties. It can be applied with beneficial results over the painful area to relieve intense headache.

(ii) Betel leaf juice is credited with diuretic properties. Its juice, mixed with dilute milk and sweetened slightly, helps in easing urination.

Reference: Raghu - 6.64, Ṛtu - 5.5, Śṛngāratilakam - 3, Puṣpavānavilāsa - 7

Tāmra (ताम्र)

Meaning/ Scientific term: Copper (Cu)

Description: It is an element of periodic table with symbol of Cu and atomic number 29. It is a ductile metal with very high thermal and electrical conductivity. Its melting point is 1083.0°C (1356.15 K, 1981.4°F) and colour: red/orange to the Roman era. Copper was principal mined on Cyprus, hence the origin of the name of the metal as Cyprium, "metal of Cyprus", later shortened to Cuperms. The 38 elements in groups 3 through 12 of the periodic table are called "transition metals". As with all metals, the transition elements are both ductile and malleable, and conduct electricity and heat.

Reference: Raghu - 5.70, 6.18, Abhi - 3.19, 6.2, Ṛtu - 6.17

Taranga (तरंग)

Meaning/ Scientific term: Wave

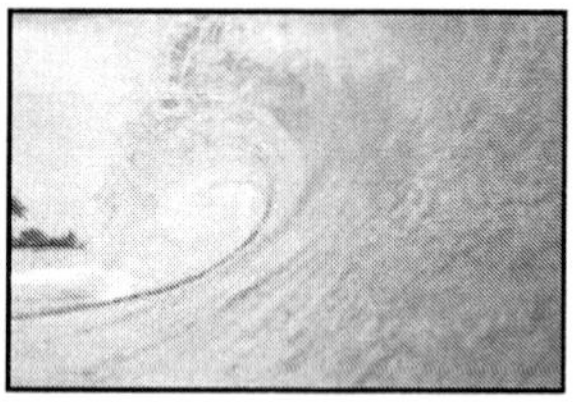

Description: A wave is a sudden increase in heat or energy that spreads out from an earthquake or explosion.

Wave is the form in which things such as sound, light and radio signals travel.

A wave is a sudden increase in a particular activity or type of behaviours, especially an undesirable or unpleasant air.

Reference: Raghu - 6.26, 7.36, 16.36, 16.78, Abhi - 3.5, Ṛtu - 3.17

Taru (तरु)

Meaning/ Scientific term: Tree

Description: Woody perennial plant typically with a single stem or trunk growing in a considerable height and bearing lateral branches.

Reference: Mālā - 1.8, 3.6, Vik - 3.21, Abhi - 1.30, 4.10, 6.20, Ṛtu - 1.24

Taru Valka (तरु वल्क)

Meaning/ Scientific term: Bark of a Tree

Description: The tough outermost layers of trunk and branches of woody plants or a tree. It refers to all the tissues outside of the vascular cambium. It overlays the wood. Products used by people that are derived from bark include: spices and other flavorings, tannin, resin, latex, medicines, poisons, various hallucinatory chemicals and cork. Bark has been used to make cloths, canoes, ropes and used as a surface for paintings and map making. A number of plants are also grown for their attractive or interesting bark colorations and surface textures or their bark is used as landscape texture.

Reference: Raghu - 8.11

Teja (तेज)

Meaning/ Scientific term: Power

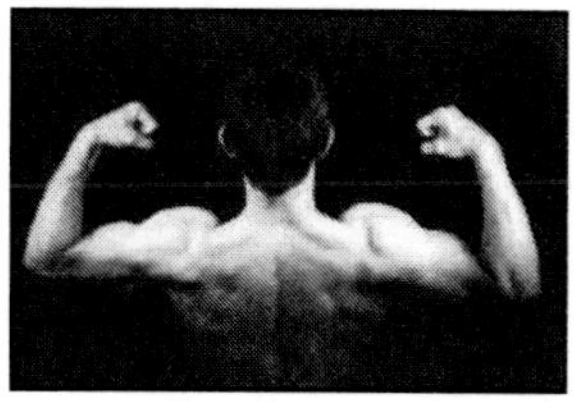

Description: Human power (human physical power) is timed rate of work done by a human. Most humans can exert only less than one-half horsepower for a duration of a few minutes. World records of power performance by humans are of interest to work planners and work-process engineers. The average level of human power that can be maintained over a certain duration of time, say over the extent of one minute or one hour is interesting to engineers designing work operations in industry.

Power is a measure of an entity's ability to control its environment, including the behavior of other entities. The term authority is often used for power perceived as legitimate by the social structure. Power can be seen as evil or unjust, but the exercise of power is accepted as endemic to humans as social beings. Often, the study of power in a society is referred to as politics.

Reference: Raghu - 2.7, 3.15, 4.31, 4.49, 6.47, 8.4, 10.30, 10.54, 10.68, 10.79, 10.83, 11.1, 11.82, Abhi - 2.7, 4.2, 4, 6.6, 7.7, 15, 27, Raghu - 14.65, 15.3, 35, 17.34, 18.40, 19.1, Mālā - 1.12, Vik - 5.20, Nalo - 1.19

Toya (तोय)

Meaning/ Scientific term: Water (H_2O)

Description: See Ambha

Reference: Kumara - 1.1, Raghu - 8.95, 17.22, 18.37, 15.65, 15.67, Vik - 1.15, Megha - 20, Ṛtu - 1.11, 2.3, 2.16, 2.20, 2.22, 2.27, 3.21

Tṛṇa (तृण)

Meaning/ Scientific term: Grass

Description: Grasses, or more technically graminoids, are monocotyledonous, usually herbaceous plants with narrow leaves growing from the base. They include the "true grasses", of the Poaceae (or Gramineae) family, as well as the sedges (Cyperaceae) and the rushes (Juncaceae). The true grasses include cereals, bamboo and the grasses of lawns (turf) and grassland. Sedges include many wild marsh and grassland plants, and some cultivated ones such as water chestnut (Eleocharis dulcis) and papyrus sedge (Cyperus papyrus). Uses for graminoids include food (as grain, sprouted grain, shoots or rhizomes), drink (beer, whisky), pasture for livestock, thatch, paper, fuel, clothing, insulation, construction, sports turf, basket weaving and many others.

Reference: Ṛtu - 1.25, 4.7, Puṣpavānavilāsa -13

Tūn (तून)

Meaning/ Scientific term: Arrow

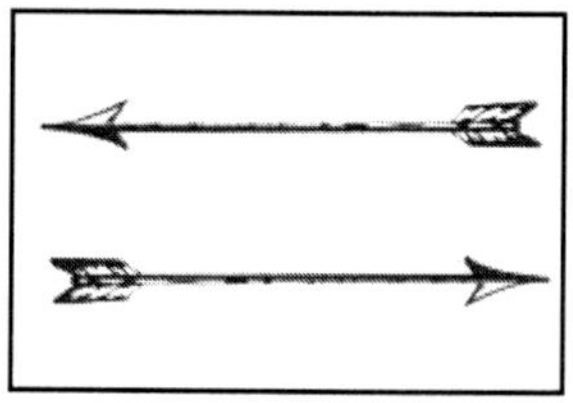

Description: This is a sharp pointed head, designed to be shot from a bow. In other word an arrow is a long thin weapon is sharp and pointed at one end and which often has feathers at the other end.

Reference: Raghu - 9.63, 57

Tusār/Tuhina (तुषार / तुहिन)

Meaning/ Scientific term: Ice

Description: Ice is water frozen into the solid state. Usually ice is the solid phase of the water. This is the most abundant of the varying solid phases on the Earth's surface. It can appear transparent or opaque bluish-white color, depending on the presence of impurities or air inclusions. The addition of other materials such as soil may further alter the appearance. The most common phase transition to ice occurs when liquid water is cooled below 0°C at standard atmospheric pressure. It can also deposit from vapour with no intervening liquid phase, such as in the formation of frost. Ice appears in nature in forms of precipitation snowflakes, hail, glaciers, pack ice, and entire polar ice caps. It is an important component of the global climate, and plays an important role in the water cycle. Furthermore, ice has numerous cultural applications, from ice cooling of drinks to winter sports and the art of ice sculpting.

Reference: Kumāra - 1.6, Raghu - 2.13, Ṛtu - 1.6, 3.15, 4.2, 5.3

U

Udaka (उदक)

Meaning/ Scientific term: Water (H_2O)

Description: *See* Ambha

Reference: Raghu - 7.40, Abhi - 1, 3, 4, Ṛtu-2.13

Ulkā (उल्का)

Meaning/ Scientific term: Meteorite

Description: A meteorite is a large piece of rock or metal from space that has landed of birth's surface.

Reference: Raghu - 16.12, 16.14

Upal (उपल)

Meaning/ Scientific term: Stone

Description: In geology, rock or stone is a naturally occurring solid aggregate of mincrals and/or, mineraloids. The Earth's outer solid layer, the lithosphere, is made of rock. In general rocks are of three types, namely, igneous, sedimentary, and metamorphic. The scientific study of rocks is called petrology, and petrology is an essential component of geology. Rocks are generally classified by mineral and chemical composition, by the texture of the constituent particles and by the processes that formed them. These indicators separate rocks into igneous, sedimentary, and metamorphic. They are further classified according to particle size. The use of rocks has had a huge impact on the cultural and technological development of the human race. Rocks have been used by humans and other hominids for more than two million years. Lithic technology marks some of the oldest and continuously used technologies. The mining of rocks for their metal ore content has been one of the most important factors of human advancement, which has progressed at different rates in different places in part because of the kind of metals available from the rocks of a region.

The prehistory and history of civilization is classified into the Stone Age, Bronze Age, and Iron Age. Although the stone age has ended virtually everywhere, rocks continue to be used to construct buildings and infrastructure. When so used, rocks are called dimension stone.

Reference: Raghu - 15.21, Ṛtu - 2.16, Abhi-1.14

Upaplava (उपप्लव)

Meaning/ Scientific term: Calamity (Natural calamity)

Description: A calamity or disaster is the tragedy of a natural or human -made hazard that negatively affects the society at large or sourrounding environment. Natural calamity would be volcanic eruption or earthquake or storm/strong wind, severe flood etc. and human-made hazards are mass killing, bombing, poisoneous gas-lick from fertilizer industry etc.

Reference: Vik - 1.12

Urmi (उर्मि)

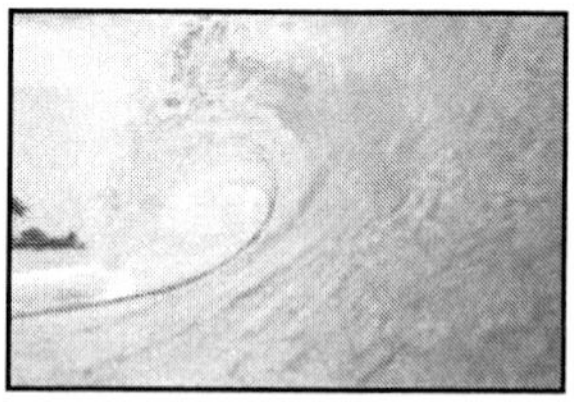

Meaning/ Scientific term: Wave in the sea/sea wave

Description: A wave is a raised mass of water on the surface of water, especially in the sea, which is caused by the wind or by tides making the surface of the water rise and fall.

Reference: Raghu - 7.54, 13.13

Uṣṇa (उष्ण)

Meaning/ Scientific term: Heat

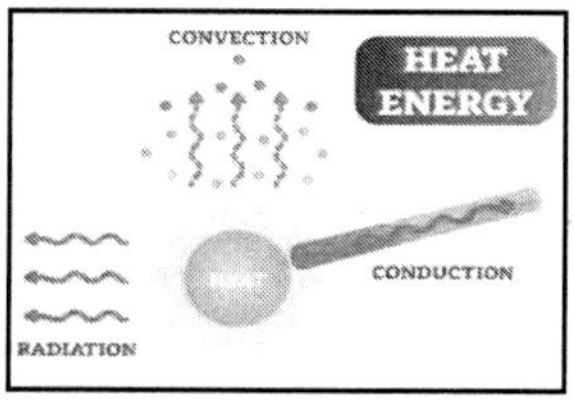

Description: When temperature of a substance or any living body is higher than normal room temperature or sourrounding temperature.

Reference: Raghu - 5.54, 8.30, 7.4, 12.62, 19.56, Abhi - 4, Mālā -5.13, Vik - 2.22, Megha 12

Uṣṇaraśmi (उष्णरश्मि)

Meaning/ Scientific term: Hot ray

Description: Heat transmitted from any heated body or substance.

Reference: Raghu - 7.33

Utpala/Nilotpala (उतपल / नीलोतपल)

Meaning/ Scientific term: Indian lotus - *Nelumbo nucifera* lotus is a kind of aquatic plant that belongs to the family Nelumbonacae.

Description: Utpala is a kind of flower which is usually appeared in the Thangka of Tibetan. It rises from mud, and is like water lily or lotus. Utpala is a symbol of the pure. Several traditional deities of Tibet including Tara have been depicted holding Utpala flowers in hands. Tara is a famous deity in Buddhism and is also worshipped by Shakti-worshipping Hindus as well especially in Eastern India, e.g., Mithila.

In Sanskrit, the neuter noun Utpala has two meanings, both given by Amarakosa (a lexicon of circa. 400 AD). The first meaning is white lotus also known as kuvalaya in Sanskrit. The second meaning of utpala is a variety of medicinal plant known as 'kooth' in Hindi and 'kuṣṭham, vyādhi, paribhavyam or pāribhavyam, vapyam, pakalam' etc.

Reference: Raghu - 3.36, 6.42, 7.26, 12.86, 13.31, Ṛtu-2.2, 9, 14, 15, 3.14, 17, 19, 26, 4.9, 5.10, Megha - 28, Abhi - 1.18, Kumāra - 1.46, 4.8, 7.20, 7.81, Puṣpavānavilāsa-11, 21

V

Vahiṇ (वहि्ण)

Meaning/ Scientific term: Fire

Description: Fire is the rapid oridation of a material in the chemical process of combustion, realeating heat, light and various reaction products. The visible portion of fire is called flame and consists of glowing hot gases. Fire in its most common form can result in conflagration, which has the potential top cause physical damage through burning. Fire has been used by humans for cooking, generating heat, signaling and propulsion purposes.

Reference: Megha - 15, Raghu - 2.75, 7.55, 8.20, 13.4, 14.14, 61, 18.28, Abhi - 7.15, Ṛtu - 1.27, 6.21, Śṛngāratilakam - 17, 21

Vaidurya (वैदुर्य)

Meaning/ Scientific term: Vaidurya Mani/Cat's Eye/gemstone

Description: Cat's Eye/gemstone comes from the mineral of Chryosberyl. It is an aluminate of beryllium-a mixture of aluminum and beryllium-having traces of oxide of iron and chromium, which serve as coloring agents and give it brownish and greenish things. Cat's eye is found in many colours. Cat's eye has white lines over it and looks similar to the eye of a cat. Cat's eye gemstone is South India, Cylon, Brazil, China and many other countries. Cat's eye is found in yellow, black, dark or smoky green, and white. The only thing common to all shades is the band of light moving across the stone, the chatoyance, gem having a white band of light is supposed to be best. Cat's-eye shines like the eye of a cat in darkness, but it does not shine in total darkness.

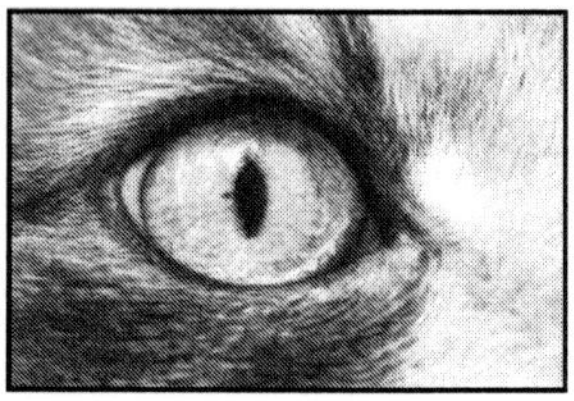

Reference: Ṛtu - 2.5, Megha - 16

Vaidya (वैद्य)

Meaning/ Scientific term: Ayurvedic Physician

Description: In Sanskrit 'Vaidya' means "one who knows". A Physician who follows the Ayurvedic system of medicine to cure people.

Reference: Mālā - 4

Vakragati (वक्रगति)

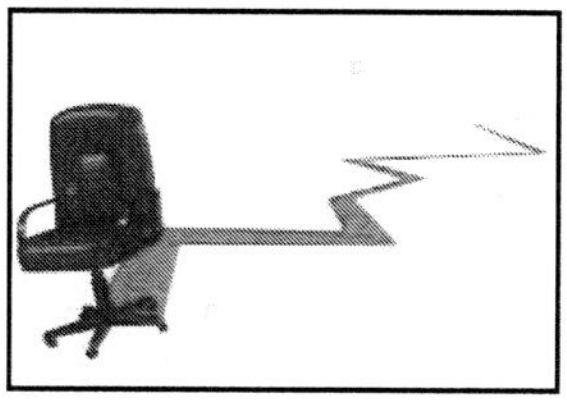

Meaning/ Scientific term: Zigzag movement

Description: Zigzag movement of a moving body or living entity means abrupt or unplanned change or shift in position or direction when going from one place to another.

Reference: Ṛtu - 2.13

Valkala (वल्कल)

Meaning/ Scientific term: Bark

Description: *See* Taru Valka

Reference: Raghu - 12.8, 14.82, 18.26, Abhi - 1.14, 1.19, 1.30, 2.13, 6.17

Vālmiki/Vālmika (वाल्मिकी / वाल्मिक)

Meaning/ Scientific term: Termite (*termites*)

Description: The termites are a group of ensocial insects usually classified as the taxonomic rank of order hoptera. Termites are small, soft-bodied insect which feed on wood and lives in colonies in large nests of earth. Original Latin terms 'woodworm'.

Reference: Raghu - 14.58, 14.79, 15.11, 15.37, 15.64, 15.69, 15.80, Megha (Purva) - 15, Abhi - 7.11

Vāna (वाण)

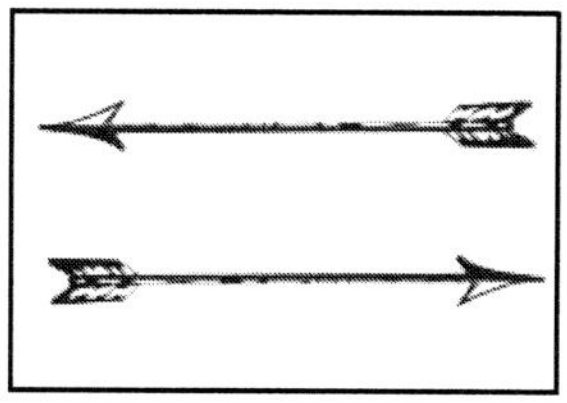

Meaning/ Scientific term: Arrow

Description: *See* Sara

Reference: Raghu - 11.26, 12.96, Mālā - 2.13, 4.12, Vik - 2, 5, 5.7, Abhi- 1, 2, 3.1, 3.3, 4, Śṛngāratilakam - 1, 8

Vanarāji/Van/Vanasthali (वनराजि / वन / वनस्थलि)

Meaning/ Scientific term: Forest

Description: A forest or woodland is a vast area found in nature with a high density of plants and trees. Forest can be found in all regions capable of sustaining tree growth, at altitude up to the tree line, except where natural fire frequency or other disturbance is too high, or where the environment has been altered by human activity. Forests sometimes contain many tree species only within a small area (as in tropical rain forests and temperate deciduous forests), or relatively few species over large areas.

Reference: Raghu - 12.20, 13.5, 13.30, 13.38, 15.8, 15.66, 16.14, 16.19, 17.64, 17.66, 18.9, Vik - 2, 5, 5. 17, Abhi - 1.17, 2, 4, 7.12, Nalo - 4.3, 4.46, Ṛtu - 1.22, 1.26, 2.9

Vanaspati (वनस्पति)

Meaning/ Scientific term: Large old tree, the great Banyan tree: Riens bengalensis

Description: Vanaspati is large, tall, old tree or plant that has a hard wide central part i.e., trunk, branches, and leaves.

Reference: Raghu - 12.21, Abhi - 4

Varāha (वराह)

Meaning/ Scientific term: Boar — Indian wild boar - *Sus scrofa cristatus*

Description: It refers to wild boar and is a species of pig. It is the wild ancestor of the demestic pig.

Reference: Raghu - 2.17, 7.56, 9.59, Abhi - 2, Ṛtu - 1.17, Kumāra - 8.35

Vāṣpa (वाष्प)

Meaning/ Scientific term: Vapour

Description: Vapour of any liquid consists of tiny drops of that particular liquid in the air, which appears as mist. Moisture or another substance that is diffused or suspended in the air. In Physics a gaseous substance that can be made into liquid by changing pressure only.

Reference: Raghu - 6.55, 8.35, 8.43, 8.68, 14.3, 14.15, 14.84, 16.44, Mālā - 3.21, Vik - 4, 4.28, 4.29, 5.9, Abhi - 4, 4.6, 4.15, 6.9, 6.22, 7.23, 7.25, Megha - 12

Vastu (वस्तु)

Meaning/ Scientific term: Substance; Matter

Description: Physical substance or material that which occupies some space and has measurable mass.

Reference: Raghu - 5.18, 17.67, Vik - 1.2, Abhi - 1.21

Vasudhā/Vasundharā/Vasumati (वसुधा / वसुन्धरा / वसुमती)

Meaning/ Scientific term: Earth

Description: Earth is the third planet from the Sun and the densest and fifth-largest of the eight planets in the Solar System. It is also the largest of the Solar System's four terrestrial planets. It is sometimes referred to as the World, the Blue Planet, or by its Latin name, Terra. Home to millions of species including humans, Earth is currently the only astronomical body where life is known to exist. The planet formed 4.54 billion years ago, and life appeared on its surface within a billion years. Earth's biosphere has significantly altered the atmosphere and other abiotic conditions on the planet, enabling the proliferation of aerobic organisms as well as the formation of the ozone layer which, together with Earth's magnetic field, blocks harmful solar radiation, permitting life on land. The physical properties of the Earth, as well as its geological history and orbit, have allowed life to persist during this period. The planet is expected to continue supporting life for at least another 500 million years. Earth is a terrestrial planet, meaning that it is a rocky body, rather than a gas giant like Jupiter. It is the largest of the four solar terrestrial planets in size and mass. Of these four planets, Earth also has the highest density, the highest surface gravity, the strongest magnetic field, and fastest rotation. It also is the only terrestrial planet with active plate tectonics.

Reference: Vik - 1.17, Raghu - 12.30, 16.28, 18.22, Abhi - 1, 1.23, 1.24, 6.24, 7.33

Vāyu (वायु)

Meaning/ Scientific term: Air

Description: Air is the name given to atmosphere used in breathing and photosynthesis. Dry air contains roughly (by volume) 78.09% nitrogen, 20.95% oxygen, 0.93% argon, 0.039% carbon dioxide and small amounts of other gases. Air also contains a variable amount of water vapour, on average around 1%. While air content and atmosphere pressure varies at different layers, air suitable for the survival of terrestrial plants and terrestrial animals is known only to be found in Earth's troposphere and artificial atmospheres. Air is mainly composed of nitrogen, oxygen, and argon, which together constitute the major gases of the atmosphere. The remaining gases are often refered to as trace gases, among which are the greenhouse gases such as water vapour, carbon dioxide, methane, nitrous oxide, and ozone. Filtered air includes trace amounts in an unfiltered air sample, including dust, pollen and spores, sea spray, and volcanic ash. Various industrial pollutants also may be present, such as chlorine (elementary or incompounds), fluorine compounds, elemental mercury, and sulfer compounds such as sulfer dioxide [SO_2].

Reference: Raghu - 8.90, 10.82, 11.28, 12.85, 14.12, 16.25, 16.36, 19.15, 19.53, Abhi - 7.6, Ṛtu - 5.3, Abhi -7.12, Puṣpavānavilāsa - 23

Vidyut (विद्युत)

Meaning/ Scientific term: Electricity

Description: Electricity is a form of energy resulting from the existence of charged particles, either statically as a build-up of charge or dynamically as a current. Electricity can be carried by wires and is used by heating and lightning, and to provide power for machines.

Reference: Raghu - 1.36, 6.5, 17.16, Mālā - 3.21, Vik - 5.16, Śruto - 14

Vihangam/Khaga (विहंगम / खग)

Meaning/ Scientific term: Bird

Description: A bird is a warm-blooded animal with feathers and wings that lays eggs: and is usually able to fly. In case of bird eggs are laid by females and incubated for a time that varies-according to the spices; simple young hatches from each egg.

Reference: Vik - 4, 5.2, 5.5, Nalo - 1.22

Vijan (विजन)

Meaning/ Scientific term: Circulation of air

Description: *See* Vyājan

Reference: Vik - 2

Vitapa (विटप)

Meaning/ Scientific term: Tree

Description: A tree is a perennial woody plant. It is most often defined as woody plant that has many secondary branches supported clear of the ground on a single main stem or trunk with clear apical dominance. Trees show a varity of growth forms, leaf type and shape, bark characterities and reproductive organs.

Reference: Raghu - 8.47, Vik - 2.8, 4, Abhi - 1.30, 3, 6, Ṛtu - 1 .24, 2.29

Vivasvān/Vivasvatā (विवस्वान / विवस्वता)

Meaning/ Scientific term: Sun

Description: *See* Tapan

Reference: Raghu - 7.60, 10.30, 15.45, Kumāra -1.16, Raghu - 1.11

Vṛhspati (वृहष्पति)

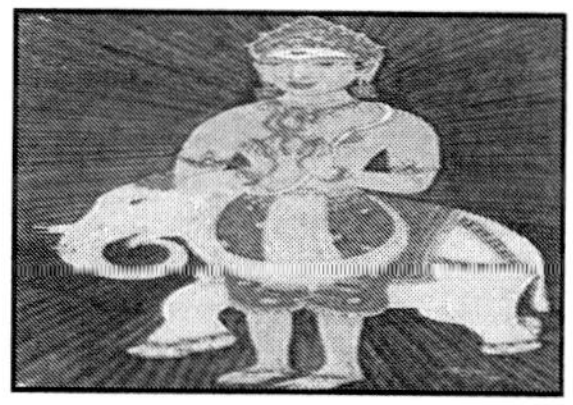

Meaning/ Scientific term: Name of a day according to Bengali calendar

Description: Brhaspati "lord of prayer or devotion", often written as Brihaspati or Bruhaspati, also known as Brahmanaspati and Deva-guru (guru of the gods), is the name of a Vedic deity. He is considered the personification of piety and religion, and the chief 'offerer of prayers and sacrifices to the gods' (Sanskrit: Purohita), with whom he intercedes on behalf of humankind. He is described of yellow or golden colour and holding the following divine attributes: a stick, a lotus and beads. He presides over "Guru-var" or Thursday. In later Hindu Theology, he is the guru of the Devas and the arch-nemesis of Shukracharya, the guru of the Danavas. He is also known as Ganapati (leader of the group [of planets]), and Guru (teacher), the god of wisdom and eloquence, to whom various works are ascribed. Hindu Mythology talks about two categories of demigods - Devas (Good) and Asuras (Evil). Brihaspati is the Guru of Devas. Symbolically he is considered as the guiding deity of the good forces. In Indian astrology, Brihaspati represents planet Jupiter and symbolically represents the Guru/Guide. Mythologically Brihaspathi is the preceptor (Guru) of the Divine aspects (Sura) of the Universe.

Reference: Raghu - 13.76

Vyāghra (व्याघ्र)

Meaning/ Scientific term: Tiger (*Panthera tigris*)

Description: The tiger, a member of the Felidae family, is the largest of the four "big cats" in the genus Panthera. The tiger is native to much of eastern and southern Asia, and is an apex predator and an obligate carnivore. The larger tiger subspecies are comparable in size to the biggest extinct felids, reaching up to 3.3 metres (11 ft) in total length, weighing up to 300 kilograms (660 pounds), and having canines upto 4 inches long, aside from their great bulk and power, their most recognisable feature is a pattern of dark vertical stripes that overlays near-white to reddish-orange fur, with lighter underparts. The most numerous tiger subspecies is the Bengal tiger, while the largest is the Siberian tiger. Tigers have a lifespan of 10-15 years in the wild, but can live longer than 20 years in captivity. They are highly adaptable and range from the Siberian taiga to open grasslands and tropical mangrove swamps i.e., in Sundarban areas. They are territorial and generally solitary animals, often requiring large contiguous areas of habitat that support their prey demands. This coupled with the fact that they are indigenous to some of the more densely populated places on earth, has caused significant conflicts with humans. Three of the nine subspecies of modern tiger have gone extinct, and the remaining six are classified as endangered. The primary direct causes are habitat destruction, fragmentation, and hunting. Historically, tigers have existed from Mesopotamia and the Caucasus throughout most of South and East Asia. Today, the range of the species is radically reduced. All surviving species are under formal protection, yet poaching, habitat destruction, and inbreeding depression continue to threaten the tigers. Tigers have featured prominently in ancient mythology and folklore, and continue to be depicted in modern films and literature. Tigers appear on many flags and coats of arms, as mascots for sporting teams, and as the national animal of several Asian nations, including India.

Reference: Raghu - 9.63, 12.37, 16.15

Vyājan (व्याजन)

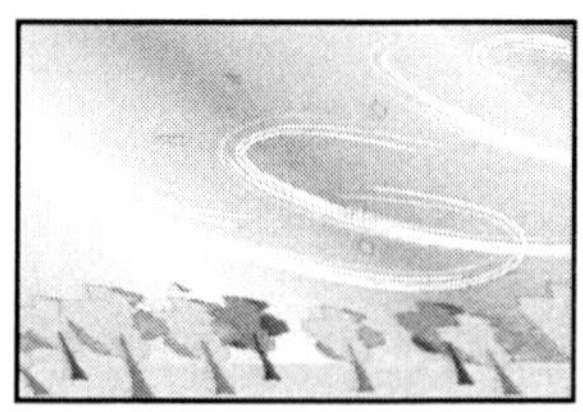

Meaning/ Scientific term: Circulation of air

Description: Circulation of air means, large-scale movement of air from one place to another nearest place by using motorized fan or hand-fan and due to this movement, heat is distributed on the surface of the Earth.

Reference: Raghu - 9.66

Vyom (वोम)

Meaning/ Scientific term: Sky

Description: The sky is the part of the atmosphere or of outer space visible from the surface of any astronomical objects. During day time sky of earth has the appearance of a deep surface because of the airs scattering of sunlight. The sky is sometimes defined as the denser gaseous use of a planet's atmosphere. At night the sky has the appearance of a black surface or region scattered with stars.

Reference: Raghu - 4.29, 12.85, 19.51, Vik - 2.1, Abhi - 6, Ṛtu - 2.2, 3.21, 3.22, 3.4

Y

Yojan/Yojana (योजन)

Meaning/ Scientific term: Unit to measure the distance in between two places

Description: A Yojana (Sanskrit) is a Vedic measure of distance used in ancient India. The exact measurement is disputed amongst scholars with distances being given between 6 to 15 kilometers (4 to 9 miles).

The length of the Yojana varied depending on the different standards adopted by different Indian astronomers. It was taken to be the distance covered by an ox cart in one day. In the Surya Siddhanta of the 5th century, for example, a Yojana was equivalent to 5 miles, and the same was true for Aryabhata's Aryabhatiya. By the time of Paramesvara in the 14th century, the Yojana was more than 1.5 times larger than it was in Aryabhata's time, thus a Yojan was equivalent to at least 8 miles by Paramesvara's time.

Reference: Nalo - 4.15

Bibliography

Balsubramaniam, R., in *Metallurgy in India- A Retrospective* edited by P. Ramachandra Rao and N.G. Goswami. National Metallurgical Laboratory, International Publisher. New Delhi, 2001, pp.104-13.

Bandyopadhyay, Alakananda, Scientific Studies in the Kālidāsa in Journal of the Deptt. of Sanskrit, R.B.U., Vol.XVII, 2009-2010, pp.190-210.

Banerjee, Suresh Ch., Kālidāsa Koṣa, Varanasi, 1968.

Banerjee, Suresh Ch., A Companion to Sanskrit Literature, Motilal Banarasidas, 1971.

Banerjee, Suresh Chandra, A Layman's Guide to Sanskrit Literature, AMBE Books, 1997.

Biswas, Arun Kumar, Vaidurya, Marakata and Other Beryl Family Gem Minerals, Etymology and Traditions in Ancient India, Indian Journal of History of Science, Vol. 29, No. 2, 1994, pp, 139-154.

Biswas, Arun Kumar and Jagatpati Sarkar. Kālidās-Sāhitye Vijnāna-Cetanā, Jnān O Vijnān, 55. (5), May 2002- pp, 200-205; 55, (6), June 2001 pp.254-259.

Biswas, Arun Kumar and Sulekha Biswas. Minerals and Metals in Ancient India, Volume II, Literary Evidences, Specially Chapter Seven, D.K. Printworld Pvt. Ltd, New Delhi, 1996, pp, 69-123 specially 81-89,

Chaklader, H.C., The Geography of Kālidāsa, Kolkata, 1963.

Chattopadhyaya, Debiprasad, Science and Society in Ancient India, Research India Publication. Calcutta 1979, Chapter 11 entitled 'Counter-Ideology' contains remarks on Brahmagupta and Al-Biruni, pp, 355-360.

Collinis, Mark, The Geographical Data of Raghuvaṁsa and the Daśakumāracarita, Leipzig, 1907.

Dwivedi, Rewa Prasad, (ed) Kālidāsa-Granthavali, B.H.U. 1986.

Laha, Satyacaran, Kālidāser Pākhi, (in Bengali) Kalikātā, 1934 with an appendix in the list of birds mentioned by Kālidāsa and an index.

Laha, Satyacharan, Pākhir Kathā, A Treatise on Orinthology with special reference to the birds mentioned in the Kālidāsa's Sanskrit works, 1921.

Laha, Satyacharan, Kālidāsa and the Migration of Bird, I and II, JASB, Vol.XX, 1924, N.S. pp.253-273.

Narang, Satpal, Kālidasa Bibliography.

Sastri, Gourinath, (ed) Samskrita Sahitya Sambhar, Vol. 2, Calcutta, 1981.

Sastri, Gourinath, (ed) Samskrita Sahitya Sambhar, Vol. 12, Calcutta, 1982.

Tagore, Rabindranath, His poem Sekāl in the book Kṣanikā, Srāvana, 1300 B.S.

Thakur, Soumendra, Kālidāser Kāvye Phul, (in Bengali), 1960.

Upadhyaya, B. S., India in Kālidāsa, Allahabad, 1947.